JUST IN TIME!

PASTORAL PRAYERS IN PUBLIC PLACES

F. Belton Joyner Jr.

Abingdon Press

Nashville

JUST IN TIME!
PASTORAL PRAYERS IN PUBLIC PLACES

This book is printed on acid-free paper.

Library of Congress Cataloging-in-Publication Data

Joyner, F. Belton.
  Pastoral prayers in public places / F. Belton Joyner Jr.
    p. cm. -- (Just in time!)
  ISBN 0-687-49567-9 (binding: adhesive : alk. paper)
  1. Prayers. 2. Pastoral prayers. 3. Pastoral theology. I. Title. II. Just in time! (Nashville, Tenn.)
  BV245.J69 2006
  264'.13—dc22

                                                                    2005022943

06 07 08 09 10 11 12 13 14 15—10 9 8 7 6 5 4 3 2 1

MANUFACTURED IN THE UNITED STATES OF AMERICA

To Toni

who prays with me every day

CONTENTS

Contents

Contents

INTRODUCTION

R ay said that he was asked to pray at the dedication of his small town's new sewer plant. Frank reported that a local church wanted him to pray at the first use of its sidewalk. Diane mentioned a church member who wanted prayer at the burial of the family's pet iguana. (Someone else, she was told, would be providing the music.)

Pastors, expected to pray or preach at a moment's notice, are often put into situations in which prayer is difficult. The difficulty might be the occasion (death from a suicide), or the setting (the scene of an accident), or the tensions (an accusation of sexual abuse), or the routine (yet another family reunion). In truth, there are times when a pastor might feel inclined to follow the injunction of Jesus to do your praying in secret (Matthew 6:6)!

This book considers some ways of praying in these hard places. Pastors (and others with a ministry of prayer) may find the pages of this volume a beginning point for their own times of praying. Some of the prayers may offer language or images that can be borrowed. In some cases, a pastor might choose to pray in the words of this book. In each of these cases, the prayers shared here are projected as ways to "get started" when called on to pray in a thorny situation.

One friend asked me why there should be a book of prayers when the Holy Spirit should give the pastor the words for a prayer (Romans 8:26). A book of prayers will never contain all that goes on in a conversation with God, but I shall miss many of God's blessings if I put a box around where the Spirit might show up! This compilation of prayers grows out of a conviction that the Holy Spirit has been present in northern Durham County, North Carolina, as these prayers were written.

Another colleague raised an important question: Are there times when it is not appropriate to pray? It is possible for dialogue with God to be cheapened by casualness or to be blocked by inattention, but the Christian tradition honors incarnation—the Word became flesh and lived among us (John 1:14)—and that presence of God has given some very unlikely places the possibilities of holiness! A pastor might well need to exercise discernment and even say no to an invitation for public prayer, but only if such praying is proposed as mere window-dressing. Even then, a prayer might serve as a corrective focus.

What about prayers in settings where persons of many faiths will be present? Even when everyone at hand is Christian, there is great variety and range of journey! How is that to be honored? When non-Christians are part of the assembly, Christian pastors do well to recall the respect to which Jesus invited us when he said, "I have other sheep that do not belong to this fold" (John 10:16a). Some Christians feel that integrity demands that they always pray "in Jesus' name." If praying in Jesus' name means to pray in the spirit and attitude and power of Jesus, then such a prayer will not seek to create undue boundaries but will move to respect where each one is on his or her path. (Our Lord was often accused of mingling with sinners.) When I thought that prayers in this book would be used in multiple-faith venues, I tried to avoid language that would keep non-Christians from having access to the throne of grace. After all, the prayer our Lord taught us (Matthew 6:9-13) contains a great deal about Jesus but does not use any words about Jesus.

These prayers blend entreaty, praise, mystery, confession, thanksgiving, and wonder. (Some hard places call for more of one than another.) Prayers are addressed to God. That observation may seem a bit basic, but we are often tempted to use address to the Almighty as an opportunity to announce to the congregation, "O Lord, please bless the youth meeting this afternoon which will meet at 5:00 instead of 6:00 as previously planned." A companion temptation is to advise the Lord of matters of which God surely is aware, "O God, as You know, on page 3 of section B of today's paper we have read of a fire at a store downtown." Having noted these potential hazards, let me ponder a bit about why a pastor might indeed tell God some things God already knows!

Public prayer is more than an exhibition of the pastor's personal prayer life. Public prayer is in behalf of that public! Although there may be one voice expressing the prayer, it is a prayer of all the people. How can someone know and feel that a prayer is his or her prayer even if someone else is speaking it? If I recognize myself when the pastor brings feelings, emotions, angers, guilts, pleas, thanksgivings before God, then I can claim that prayer as "ours," even "mine."

For example, in a prayer suggestion for use when there has been the denial of abuse, there is this line: "Our anger comes from our fear, fear of retribution, fear of continued abuse, or fear of continued false accusation." That sentence, on its own, could well pass for a word from a sermon (or counseling session) addressed not to God but to the congregation.

However, in the context of public prayer, that sentence becomes a way of helping others recognize themselves in the prayer language of the pastor, so the prayer also becomes their prayer. When I can say (as I hear a prayer), "Yeah, that's me," I can also join in the petition to God as my petition, the praise of God as my praise, the confession to God as my confession.

Another example: in a prayer with a child who is in the midst of a custody decision, a suggested prayer seems to describe the obvious to God: "(Evan) loves his mother, and he loves his father, and he is sad that they do not love each other." As the child, Evan, "eavesdrops" on these words said to God, he is more likely to see this as his prayer.

There are many forms for prayers in the hard places. The prayers in this collection sometimes call for silence, sometimes ask participants to repeat phrases, sometimes close with the Lord's Prayer. Persons who are going through trauma together might find strength in holding hands as they pray. There is a special power in kneeling when praying. There is a claim upon a prayer when all are asked to close with an "Amen." (This can be cued simply by saying, "And all God's people said . . . Amen.")

Scattered through these pages are prayers that pause in order for individuals to pray aloud, "Hear the name of those of the past whom we remember (I invite you to call those names aloud)." Some congregations have grown accustomed to these calls of joys and concerns, but in other settings such an invitation may create the silence of awkwardness. The silence itself is not bad, but the leader can temper it by alerting, in advance, one or two persons that there will be an opportunity to name persons to be remembered in prayer; those one or two persons will then be ready to speak aloud, modeling for those who are less sure.

Obviously, it is one thing to lead a prayer in a small family circle and another thing to pray through a scratchy public address system. Although the tone of voice in public prayer should not be stiff, neither should it become chatty. God is a Friend, but God is also the Almighty! Prayer is not the occasion for practicing dramatic excesses. In most circumstances, the prayer will more likely become "the prayer of the people" if the leader speaks slowly enough for the gathered group (or individual with whom one is praying) to have time to seize the words reflectively as their own. When reading a prayer, we tend to read too quickly. If the prayers of this book are read aloud, slow down! Vary the pace of reading.

The very nature of praying in hard places means that each situation is unique. (If we were in an "ordinary" place, we would more likely know what to do, what to say. The situation's distinctiveness is part of what makes it hard!) In a sense, all of our praying simply joins the prayer of our great high priest, Jesus Christ (Hebrews 4:14–5:10). This should give us great confidence when our words fall short, when our focus seems scattered, when our hearts become empty. It is no small matter to represent a people in prayer. It is no small matter to have Jesus Christ praying with us!

HOW TO USE THIS BOOK

In this collection, I have followed a common format: title of setting, description of setting, example of setting, relevant Scripture, and prayer suggestion. Let me comment on each.

Title of Setting

There are eighty prayer settings in this small volume. That means that only 87,256,918,482 have been left out! I have tried to provide illustrations that range from the likely to the hardly-ever. Finding the right way to categorize a prayer was not easy: should prayer when a pet dies go under "Family" or under "Pets"? You will find your way through the series better if you read through the entire table of contents rather than counting on what made sense to me at the time I typed the headings!

Certainly, you will have requests for prayer that do not fit these precise settings. Consider these titles as prayer ticklers, the kind of reminders that trigger your awareness that there are many junctures in life that invite prayer. I had a seminary professor who was asked if a pastor should always pray when visiting in the hospital. Mr. Haas said, "Probably not always, but if I am going to make an error about it, I should prefer to say to myself as I leave, 'I wish I had not prayed that time' rather than 'I wish I had had a prayer.' Let me err on the side of praying!"

Use these titles as entry points for your own pastoral work. (And, if the truth be told, there are situations in which persons who are not pastors will have access for praying that might be denied clergy.) The titles are intended to be starters, not exhaustive lists.

Description of Setting

These lines introduce the dimensions that make this condition one that calls for prayer. Why would the pastor go to help pick out a casket? Why would a pastor offer a prayer in a worship service that precedes high school exams? What is the role of the clergy at a civic observance?

This material is drawn in broad strokes. Volumes have been written on pastoral theological matters that I handle in one sentence. Always assume that there is more to be said (and thought and wondered) than is captured in these brief lines! One supposition I made was that these conditions are within the United States. Cultural and geographic specifications make a difference. Does your social context give you a singular set of lenses for looking at the settings for prayer?

Example of Setting

Real people inhabit our prayer worlds, so I have tried to illustrate these prayer times with stories that give the particulars. These examples are all the product of my imagination and the names of the people involved are not intended to identify real individuals.

Often in a prayer, I have used the names of my fictional characters. This personalization of a prayer helps us move from boilerplate, generic praying to acknowledgment of God's investment in each life.

The downside of these examples is that they could make it harder to adjust the prayers to similar but distinct opportunities. For example, there is a prayer for the time of bringing home a new pet. In the illustration, the pet is a snake. There are one or two sentences that are specific to bringing home a snake, "Help us connect even with this snake." but you will have to make needed adjustments for goldfish, spiders, monkeys, or Rottweiler puppies!

Relevant Scripture

Each prayer reflection includes a biblical quotation. These verses are intended primarily for the pastor (or other person) who will be leading the prayer. The biblical texts are part of our conversation with God. In some cases, the passage might be read aloud; at other times, the Scripture will be used for preparation.

Sometimes, instead of our choosing a text, a text chooses us! The implication of that is that some of these biblical images are comforting and supportive, while others are convicting and challenging. (Being in God's presence is like that!)

I have tried to pay attention to the context of the Bible selections. Longer quotations would be necessary to form the framework of the single verse (or two) that make up this portion of the format. Remember John

Wesley's sage insight that Scripture is twice inspired, once when written and once when read. What does God reveal to us in the text for this time and place?

All quotations are from the *New Revised Standard Version of the Bible*. Other translations, of course, offer alternative images and perceptions. Immersing yourself in Scripture will help you develop vocabulary and reference points for the prayers for the hard places. From time to time, in the prayers in this assortment, there are biblical allusions that will add depth for persons who know the Bible, and are also appropriate for those not familiar with biblical sources.

Prayer Suggestion

This is the heart of the book. I have tried to enter into the imaginary scenes enough to be faithful to their emotional sensitivities, their civic realities, and their raw places. You will no doubt detect certain patterns in my writing, particular ways I express myself, common configurations of language. (There! That's one! I often write in triplets!) If these styles are foreign for you, be cautious about duplicating them. It is important for me to pray this way because this is part of who I am. If it is not what flows from your core or—and I need to listen to this myself—if it does not allow all present to be a part of the prayer, be vigilant against meaningless repetition.

In almost all of the prayers, I have chosen to use *we* language. Whether there are two present or a stadium filled with thousands, the *we* word assists in making this a community prayer, not merely letting others listen in on my private conversation with God, but inviting them to hear this as their prayer too.

Speaking of inviting, while I have the floor, may I speak about a pet peeve? When calling persons to join us in praying, the encounter is best served if the leader is straightforward: "Let us pray." The tentative "Will you join me in prayer?" or the uncertain "Can we pray together?" or the unsure "Will you pray with me, please?" simply do not establish the climate of confidence that we have been told to take: "Let us therefore approach the throne of grace with boldness, so that we may receive mercy and find grace to help in time of need" (Hebrews 4:16).

I hope you find these prayers good companions for your ministry. Feel free to adapt and use them in ways that are helpful.

There are countless ways of addressing God. Many of these emerge in the immense scope of these prayers: Father, Comforter, Savior, Creator, Mother, Holy Spirit, Lord, Author of wisdom, Giver of truth, Son, Source of strength, triune God. Working within the limits of language to call on the eternal God is like trying to nail Jell-O to the wall; it might capture some of what is present, but there is always more that we miss! As I wrote these prayers, I found that two words showed up over and over again: "claim" and "presence." Indeed, there is an audacity to our claim to reach out to Almighty God, but it is precisely the presence of that God that invites us to do so. Claim the presence!

D E A T H

FUNERAL HOME—CHOICES TO BE MADE

Few settings make death more real for a family than actually sitting with a representative of a funeral home, making decisions about service and burial plans. A pastoral presence can provide support and sacred boundaries for those conversations.

Example

Mary Johnson had long expected her mother to die. Over eight difficult years, her mother slowly became less and less the person Mary had known, reduced to a non-communicating shadow of her former self. Now she has died. Mary, with a few family members and her pastor, sits down with the funeral director to plan the needed next steps.

> *Protect me, O God, for in you I take refuge.*
> *I say to the LORD, "You are my Lord;*
> *I have no good apart from you." (Psalm 16:1-2)*

Prayer

It is hard to admit, O God, that life includes death. Here we come with choices to be made that will not let us escape the reality of loss, the certainty of transition, the emptiness of these moments. Our claim is upon Your presence. Our hope is sustained in Your promise. Our trust is that You will guide us.

Clear our minds with a peace the world cannot give. Calm our anxieties with coolness for the heat of our hurt. Collect us with all those who would help us that we might move in ways which honor good memory, which unfold new possibilities, and which strengthen us for these days.

Our hours of recall are not always good, but we know that Your love is; and now in thanksgiving we accept Your guidance in the face of death as surely as You are with us in the fullness of life; through Jesus Christ our Lord. Amen.

DEATH

BEFORE THE SERVICE

The family has gathered, often from some distance; and it is time to go into the sanctuary or to some other place for the service. The ritual of this entrance can be awkward for those not accustomed to being the focus of attention, painful for those who are struggling with death's seeming power, and significant for those who see these coming moments as a final good-bye.

Example

Evan had done his best "to hold it together" as many in the family grieved openly at the death of Aunt Diane. She had always been the one "to be there" for others, and now they were here for her. Evan shuddered quietly as the signal came that it was time to go into the service. A sensitive pastor recognized this as a time for centering prayer.

Recalling your tears, I long to see you so that I may be filled with joy. I am reminded of your sincere faith, a faith that lived first in your grandmother Lois and your mother Eunice and now, I am sure, lives in you. (2 Timothy 1:4-5)

Prayer

Here we are, O God, ready to offer You praise for the life of Aunt Diane. There is praise to be given, but there is also pain to be felt. We are grateful for those who have gathered to carry part of that pain with us. We are grateful for the life that now we celebrate. We are grateful for this community of faith, which by nature is drawn by Your magnetic grace to pray, to proclaim, and to persevere.

Go with us into this service. Indeed, we claim that, in Christ Jesus, You have preceded us into this hard place. And in His name we see that victory even in our loss; in His name we hear that hallelujah even in our sadness; in His name we taste a banquet where all Your saints will gather even as now we come. Amen.

DEATH

NO FAMILY OR FRIENDS

A cemetery can be a place of uncommon bleakness when a pastor meets personnel from the funeral home for a burial of someone who is not remembered by family or friends. The pastor and those who work at the gravesite might well be the only persons present. Almost certainly, the deceased will be someone the pastor does not know in any other context.

Example

The phone rang in Pastor Christianson's office. She answered and heard the familiar voice of Carl Wynne, day manager at the community funeral home. "Reverend, we've got this man here who died at Memorial Hospital. They have no record of any family or connections. Can you meet us at Gracelawn Cemetery at 2:30 and do a service?"

Two are better than one, because they have a good reward for their toil. For if they fall, one will lift up the other; but woe to one who is alone and falls and does not have another to help. (Ecclesiastes 4:9-10)

Prayer

God, our creating Parent, You said that it was not good that we should be alone. God, our blessed Savior, You yourself were left apart in solitary prayer and in solitary suffering. God, our living Breath, You seek us; You seek us until You find us.

We gather here now, Source of all grace, because You have made us all into one family. Our brother has gone into Your closer presence, and we do not even know who would mourn this loss. This child of Yours has died, and now we are left with the questions of life's mysteries. How silly of us to think that he is unknown because we do not know him! How rich is Your love that cares for the sparrow that falls, for the lily that fades, and now for this son who returns where life began, in Your caring and watchful presence. We pray in the name of the triune God, ever in community that we might always have family. Amen.

DEATH

SUICIDE

One of the hardest pastoral responsibilities is to minister after a suicide attempt. If the death is completed, there is an added dimension of the struggle to understand and accept; if the effort is not finalized, there are issues of doubt, guilt, broken relationships.

Example

To all appearances, Ellis Van Buren had a good life, filled with business successes, strong family ties, and an active faith. Shock and disbelief rampaged through the community when people began to find out that Mr. Van Buren had taken his own life. "Why?" "Did I miss some signal?" "What could I have done to prevent it?" "Can he go to heaven if he shot himself?" "Why?" "Why?"

> Then Saul said to his armor-bearer, "Draw your sword and thrust me through with it, so that these uncircumcised may not come and thrust me through, and make sport of me." But his armor-bearer was unwilling; for he was terrified. So Saul took his own sword and fell upon it. (1 Samuel 31:4)

Prayer

O God, if we knew why, we would name it before You! Hear our plea for help; hear our plea for hope. We confess that we do not grasp the depths which drive one of Your children to end the life You began. We confess that faint stirrings of guilt, soft wondering about our own inattentions, and a simple unease all groan within us. Grant us a grace which will be sufficient for our own broken and breaking places.

We thank You for Your love which is not constrained by the boundaries of life and death. Into Your tender presence, we commend our brother. Even now, heal him by a gift that always comes to us undeserved. Even now, receive him as a child who trusted his Parent's final tomorrow, all of which we reach to grasp; through Jesus Christ our Lord. Amen.

DEATH

NEW GRAVESTONE AT CEMETERY

The marker for a new grave is not usually installed at the cemetery until several weeks after the burial. Some of the initial work of grieving may well have been done, and the pastor can use the occasion to help survivors move to a new place of healing.

Example

Merino Valaquez was excited about the marker planned for her father's grave. "We had them carve a rose on the stone because the rose was Papa's favorite flower. He always said it bloomed when some flowers drooped. And that's the way he was!" Pastor Kirby suggested, "Why don't we all go to the cemetery and have a prayer to dedicate that stone?"

> Then Samuel took a stone and set it up between Mizpah and Jeshanah, and named it Ebenezer [that is, Stone of Help]; for he said, "Thus far the LORD has helped us." (1 Samuel 7:12)

Prayer

God of the ages, how recently we gathered here to commit to the ground your servant, Edgardo! We thank You for restoring good memories of his life among us. We thank You for promises of the gift of resurrection.

Now, Lord, we mark this place in a way to declare it a special place. With a rose that blossoms even yet, we recall a good life that reaches us even yet. With a rock that names a name, we declare that You have loved us one at a time. With this sign for our loved one, we dare to offer his memory to generations yet to come. Thank You, Lord Jesus, for walking with us when we left this place on another day, and now go with us in the gladness of new tomorrows made possible through Your grace. Amen.

DEATH

DECORATIONS AT CEMETERY

Many cemeteries allow visitors to bring special decorations for gravesites. Frequently, persons see this opportunity as a seasonal ritual—Christmas, Easter, spring, for example. These signs of memory may go on for years or just be offered occasionally. A pastor might offer to join the family on its first such visit.

Example

Barbara and Fred Bryant had been married thirty-six years when he died. When the next Christmas came, she wanted to place a small plant at the grave. "He gave me a poinsettia every Christmas we were married," she told her pastor. "Now I want to give one to him." Only the pastor and Barbara Bryant went to the cemetery as the brisk winter winds worked chills around every marker. "Will you offer a prayer, Pastor, after I put Fred's plant at his grave?"

> The flowers appear on the earth;
>   the time of singing has come,
> and the voice of the turtledove
>   is heard in our land. (Song of Solomon 2:12)

Prayer

Generous God, You have given us love, and its bounty is such that now it reaches across borders of life and death. Caring God, You have given us memory, and its gift is such that now joys of yesterday struggle to express themselves today. Creating God, You have given us plants for beauty, and their touch upon us is such that now they bring forth yet again a glimpse of a yes in the midst of life's sadness.

With thanksgiving, we remember the Christmas after Christmas that Barbara and Fred spent together. With joy, we remember the birth of Jesus and await His coming again. And in these times in-between—between Christmas past and Christmas now and Christmas yet to be—receive this plant as a celebration of Your presence in this hard place and as a gratitude for the years when such a plant meant so much. We dare to pray this because of Jesus Christ. Amen.

C O U R T

CITIZENSHIP

Changing one's citizenship is one way of moving into new relation-ships, even into another identity. Putting this important moment within the context of the Christian faith gives a shaping dimension to citizenship.

Example

Kwang-Jin Jung had wondered if this day would ever come! "I bring who I am with me," he said, "but I am in a new location. This now is my home of place." Pastor Faggart was alert to the significance of the citizenship ceremony and invited Kwang-Jin Jung and family to have a prayer of celebration and responsibility. "That's who I am too," the proud new citizen-to-be had said.

> Pay to all what is due them—taxes to whom taxes are due, revenue to whom revenue is due, respect to whom respect is due, honor to whom honor is due. (Romans 13:7)

Prayer

O God, the Giver of beginnings, we praise You for giving to Your servant Kwang-Jin Jung fresh possibilities, extended hopes, and a new nation. You have given him life; and now You call him to new loyalties, new responsibilities, and new opportunities. We make no claim for the perfection of this nation; but we do make full claim upon Your presence in its work for justice, its care for the poor, and its openness to those who seek to be its people.

Keep alive in this citizen the gifts of a past and the fruits of a heritage. As he turns toward the duties of a different flag, grant him the joys of its best memories and the challenges of its weaker moments. And in all things keep him pointed toward that kingdom which knows not human boundaries and which will finally show peace and abundance to all the nations; through Jesus Christ our Lord. Amen.

COURT

CRIMINAL TRIAL

Questions of guilt and innocence may shape the ultimate spiritual needs of one who undergoes a criminal trial, but the pressures and hazards and unanticipated moments all create a basic pastoral setting: a confused, hurting, off-balance time.

Example

The charges were serious. Sylvia Pilaster said she had been misunderstood: what some took for illegal assault had really been self-defense when her home was being invaded. "You don't use a snow shovel to hit a young teen before he has a chance to turn and leave, but that is what she did," the prosecutor said. "Ms. Pilaster had no way to know this intruder's intent when he showed up on her screened porch," the defense lawyer stated. Out of jail on bond, Sylvia Pilaster wanted her pastor to pray.

> To do righteousness and justice
> is more acceptable to the LORD than sacrifice. (Proverbs 21:3)

Prayer

Everything seems to be coming unglued, O Lord. To some, our yes sounds like a no, and our no sounds like a yes. Tomorrow holds we know not what. And today holds enough troubles to suffice for a season. But we look on that hill far away, and the cross is still empty. We look into that tomb beside the useless rock, and the tomb is still empty. It's Your presence with us now that gives us power that is not written by human hand or decided by human thought. You who see the heart as quickly as others see the hand, flush with forgiveness the sinful places of our lives and love us enough that we shall be able to forgive those who wrong us or seek to wrong us.

Be with those to whom our society has entrusted judgments of right and wrong, and when those decisions please You, we give You thanks, and when those decisions make sad your heart, grant us grace to live toward righteousness, which we have seen in and claim through Jesus Christ our Lord. Amen.

COURT

SENTENCING HEARING

Once a court's guilty verdict has been heard, some persons are disappointed, shocked, angered; others feel justified, pleased, even triumphant. In each case, the hearing to determine an appropriate sentence is high in emotion and expectation.

Example

Odell Paschal knew that he had been found guilty. "Why don't I feel guilty?" he asked the Reverend Ms. Swanson. "I know I did wrong, but I never thought it would come to this. I could even be put in prison! What about my family? Maybe that is what I feel guilty about—leaving them for prison—not for this technical violation of some obscure tax law!" Ms. Swanson knew it was not a moment for her to speak. "I guess I'm in denial," added Mr. Paschal. "Will you pray for me?"

> *The spirit of the Lord GOD is upon me,*
> *because the LORD has anointed me;*
> *he has sent me to bring good news to the oppressed,*
> *to bind up the brokenhearted,*
> *to proclaim liberty to the captives,*
> *and release to the prisoners. (Isaiah 61:1)*

Prayer

Gracious God, these hours ahead of us are filled with anxiety, and our anxiety is filled with despair. Thoughts and emotions flood our hearts, so we pray that there be a place in our hearts for You. Come with that strange stillness that flows from Your presence even when we feel an absence.

You have felt pain, O God. In Your Son You know what it is to turn to another and say, "Take care of my mother." Some of the shatteredness felt here is not of self but of those who have been wounded and who now face the possibility of long days and empty nights without one who is loved. Now, may Your will be done: the will to forgive, the will to heal, the will to serve, the will to continue. May Your will be done; through Your Son, Jesus Christ. Amen.

C O U R T

For Judges

The decisions that must be made by a judge affect the lives of both those in the courtroom and others far beyond. Judges try to keep "the law" as a level playing field. Personal views can be in tension with legal realities. There is the temptation to arbitrary use of power. This is not an easy role.

Example

After Kalamba Kanyangare was elected judge, he knew that the pressures and stresses of his life would be many. He was not the kind of man who thought he could "leave it in the courtroom." Judge Kanyangare wanted the prayer support of his church. "Pastor," he asked, "can this be a prayer not just for me, but for all judges?"

> Then the LORD raised up judges, who delivered them out of the power of those who plundered them. (Judges 2:16)

Prayer

O God, Who is the Judge of the living and the dead, we pray this day for those who are called to make judgments in the civil affairs of Your created order. Grant them a wisdom born not of vengeance, but of compassion. Grant them a love of justice born not of arrogance, but of righteousness. Grant them a courage born not of power, but of truth.

We confess, God of mercy, that our human law sometimes falls short of divine will. We confess our own desire sometimes to live in ways contrary to Your purposes. We confess that each of us has sinned and fallen short of Your glory. Even so, O Lord, let the judges of this land be women and men who grasp Your gift of new beginnings, Your hope that the people be protected, and Your call for ears tuned to Your tomorrow. And finally we make our accountability to You through the saving power of the Lord Jesus Christ. Amen.

S C H O O L

GRADUATION

Completing each stage of formal education is an achievement to be acknowledged. Sometimes it represents a fresh start; sometimes it represents closure of relationships; sometimes it contains disappointment; sometimes it contains a sense of accomplishment. Seldom is it "business as usual."

Example

Peter Braxton was one of four high school seniors who happily put on cap and gown for his congregation's Senior Recognition Service. Because Peter was the first member of his family to complete high school, Pastor Bergland had helped the proud parents celebrate with a time of prayer at the home. Now Peter brought all of those emotions to this traditional worship service at Logan Memorial Church.

*And Jesus increased in wisdom and in years, and in divine and human favor.
(Luke 2:52)*

Prayer

O God, Author of all wisdom, Giver of all truth, Seeker of all servants, we thank You for the times of life that mark Your continuing goodness. We are grateful for these believers, young in their faith and early in their journey, who have been open to study and learning and who now gain graduation toward tomorrows that will take them in many directions, but never from Your presence.

For friendships formed, we give You thanks. For obstacles overcome, we give You thanks. For faith sustained, we give You thanks. For creativity expressed, we give You thanks. For brokenness healed, we give You thanks. And for the "not yet" places of life, we give You thanks. All of this we pray through the One who sat among the teachers and Who Himself grew in wisdom, even Jesus Christ our Lord. Amen.

SCHOOL

BEFORE AN EXAM

Days of testing can be stressful, for teachers and for students. Various states have instituted end-of-grade exams or standard requirements for graduation. Many learners, preparing for college, take SAT or similar tests. A teacher wonders: have I taught well? A student wonders: have I learned well?

Example

Wanisha Foley and Jessica Smith were getting ready for placement exams. Although they had been good students (nothing brilliant, but nothing disastrous), they feared the hours they would now spend poring over quirky math problems, sorting out language loopholes, and writing the dreaded essay. Bryan Young, their pastor, knew that on Sunday many in the congregation would be filled with the same anxieties.

For [God] will command his angels concerning you
to guard you in all your ways. (Psalm 91:11)

Prayer

Come into our hearts, Lord Jesus. Come into the places of turmoil and bring peace. Come into the places of rest and bring energy. Come into the places of tension and bring calm. Come into the places of weakness and bring strength. Come into the places of casualness and bring purpose. Come into our hearts, Lord Jesus.

Creator God, this day we bring ourselves to You as we are. We do some things well and sometimes our best efforts fail. But now, in the face of things that will test us, in the hours ahead that will reach inside us, in the pressures that will build around us, we pray for grace sufficient that we might offer the fullness of who we are. Take away the strains that would work against us, but be present in the efforts that will call forth our best, until finally we recall with joy that our value is not in passing or failing, but in Your willingness to claim us as Your children; through Jesus Christ our Lord. Amen.

S C H O O L

NO TO COLLEGE

Sometimes when students decide not to go to college, their families are in disarray: hurt, disappointed, and chagrined. Also, there are high school graduates who have recently learned that they will not be accepted into schools of their choice. An alert pastor can support students and families in these times.

Example

Oswald (just call me "Ozzie") McArthur told his dad, "I'm not going to college if I can't get in Lowell. I'll just keep my job at Burger Beast until something else comes along." Mr. McArthur, a single parent, felt all the burden o trying to "talk sense" into Ozzie. He asked Pastor Armistead to help him and Ozzie deal with the impasse. When the pastor showed up at the McArthur home, the tension of the family debate was obvious.

> In the morning sow your seed, and at evening do not let your hands be idle; for you do not know which will prosper, this or that, or whether both alike will be good. (Ecclesiastes 11:6)

Prayer

And our Lord said, "Peace to this house!" God of love, Giver of good tomorrows, we thank You for the path that now brings Ozzie to times of decision. You have blessed him with a caring parent; You have blessed him with completed school; You have blessed him with a ready mind. Now bless him with patience, with purpose, and with peace.

Clear within each of us space to hear what we say to one another. Most of all, clear within each of us space to hear what You would say to us. We offer our disappointments as the ground for new beginnings You might give; we offer our uncertainties as the sign of our openness to Your leading; we offer our disagreements as a mark that You are in the midst of our lives to stretch us, to claim us, and to fulfill us. Bless this home with the sunshine of a love that passing clouds might sometimes hide, all of which we claim through Your Son, our Lord, Jesus Christ. Amen.

SCHOOL

SCHOOL FIGHTS

Schools are not exempt from the angers and traumas that often stretch human relationships to the breaking point. Heated words, fights, and even weapons can become the expressions of this brokenness. When distress comes to the school, distress comes to the entire community. It can be a time for pastoral triage!

Example

When Devon Brookshire left for school, she did not expect to witness a stabbing in the student parking lot. A classmate (Devon knew him only as Terry) and a senior Devon did not know began arguing over who was responsible for a fender bender. At the height of the dispute, many students gathered around. Suddenly, Terry slipped a knife from under his shirt and slashed his opponent. Blood and shrieks amplified the crisis as friends jumped into the fray. Before the skirmish was over, seven students were wounded, one seriously.

> It is honorable to refrain from strife,
> but every fool is quick to quarrel. (Proverbs 20:3)

Prayer

When places of safety become places of horror, reach us again with steadfast love, O God. When days of routine become days of tragedy, reach us again with steadfast love, O God. When school is marked more by lesions than by lessons, reach us again with steadfast love, O God.

O God, our Loving Parent, we confess our own hearts of anger. Put a wall of grace around us to keep us from hurting others or ourselves. O God, our Caring Companion, we confess our own quick triggers of emotion. Put a wall of peace around us to keep us from hating. O God, our Breathing Source, we confess our own frights and fears. Put a wall of hope around us to keep us from despair. Three-in-one God, bring salve for those who hurt so much that they hurt others. Fill us with Your yes in the face of life's no; through the Prince of Peace we pray. Amen.

S C H O O L

CHEATING

The pressure to achieve opens the door to the temptation to cheat. The power of sin in our lives can lead us to seek easy ways "to get by." The devilish challenge to see if we can do wrong without getting caught can block us from our best. Cheating is a reality in school.

Example

Bettye Mays asked her pastor, Betty Cole, to stay for a moment after youth meeting. The two often teased about having the same first name, so teen Bettye said to her pastor: "Betty 2, I need to talk with you. Now. Can we go to your study?" Once settled with Bettye in the small cube of an office, the Reverend Ms. Cole asked, "Something on your mind?" Bettye began to cry. "I have done something awful." Ms. Cole waited. "I needed an A to make Honor Roll, (Bettye's voice cracked), so I turned in a paper I copied straight off the Internet. My teacher has no idea; he gave me an A."

> My friends, if anyone is detected in a transgression, you who have received the Spirit should restore such a one in a spirit of gentleness. (Galatians 6:1a)

Prayer

Merciful God, Your child Bettye comes now with a broken heart. She has named her sin before You. She brings no pretense or excuse. She brings nothing in her hand other than a palm open to receive Your forgiving touch.

Be with her now as she gathers the courage to complete her repentance. Be with her so she does not go alone when she brings this deception to her teacher. And grant Bettye such an awareness of Your love that she finds more joy in righteousness than she does in marks of A or B. This forgiveness we see in Jesus Christ. This love we see in Jesus Christ. This righteousness we see in Jesus Christ, so we pray in His name. Amen.

S C H O O L

NEW KID ON THE BLOCK

School settings can be stressful even when familiar, but being at a new school can be especially upsetting. Changing schools can occur for lots of reasons: family move, magnet schools, grade promotion, reassignment, suspension, and special programs. Prayers in homes of such changes can give a pastoral gift to school-aged family members.

Example

On a map, it might not seem far from 316 East Third Street to 4721 Mountain View Road; but when the Pedraja family moved, it seemed like an entirely new world for the children. New neighbors. New stores. And most unsettling, new schools. Roberto and Raoul—twin brothers, sixth graders—were alternately excited and angry.

> Then one of them, whose name was Cleopas, answered him, "Are you the only stranger in Jerusalem who does not know the things that have taken place there in these days?" (Luke 24:18)

Prayer

Dear God, Raoul and Roberto need your help; they are being asked to do something that is not easy to do. You went with Abraham when he went to a new land. You went with Moses when he led Your people to a new place. You went with Peter, James, and John when they were called to leave their fishing in order to follow Jesus. Now, we ask that You go with Roberto and Raoul as they enter a new school.

Give them open spirits to make new friends. Give them calmness to make good decisions. Give them memories to make good use of the school now left behind.

If they feel alone, give them courage. If they feel overwhelmed, give them simple steps to walk. If they feel new joys, give them grateful hearts. This we pray in the name of the One who walked the lonesome valley, even Jesus Christ our Lord. Amen.

S C H O O L

New Building

The construction of a school building can be an occasion for community rejoicing (Hooray! No more overcrowding), community resentment (Why is my tax dollar putting up something for them?), or community pride (We have first-class facilities now). The setting for prayer is further complicated by concerns for appropriate church-state relations.

Example

Yvonne Tarryton drove her pastor to the dedication ceremonies for Fleetwood Junior High School. Mrs. Tarryton, a member of the school board, was in charge of planning the program and had asked the Reverend Mr. Snotherly to offer a prayer with school board members just before the public procedures.

> I am the LORD your God,
>> who teaches you for your own good,
>> who leads you in the way you should go. *(Isaiah 48:17b)*

Prayer

O God of all generations, Who loves young and old, Who gives both wisdom and experiment, we thank You for this place. We are grateful for those whose sacrifices have turned into brick and mortar, and grateful for those whose challenge has led us all to think more clearly about what it is to teach and learn.

Bless those who will teach here; give them a sense of mission that will shape their care for students. Bless those who will study here; give them a sense of intention that will give them energy for learning. Bless those who will administer the work done here; give them a larger view of wisdom that will form their decisions. And bless these members of the school board; give them the gift of oversight that they might honor Your will as they strive for Your children.

We offer Fleetwood Junior High School for the good of this community and the broader world we reach. In Your promise, we pray. Amen.

S C H O O L

TEACHERS AND ADMINISTRATORS

Our society puts a great deal of expectation on the school system. Teachers and those who serve as principals and superintendents almost always put the interests of the students above their own. What a gift for each community!

Example

When Carson Weaver decided to go into teaching, he did so remembering Ms. Caviness, Mr. Poston, Mr. Alston, and Ms. Howard—all favorite teachers of his own. They had made him feel significant. They had told him when he was wrong. They had built on his strengths to direct him toward a strong future. And that is what he wanted to do as the language arts teacher at Norton Central High. So, before the school year began, he asked Pastor Dover-Brown to meet with a group of like-minded teachers. "We need to know that people care; we need to know that God cares."

> For it is precept upon precept, precept upon precept,
> line upon line, line upon line,
> here a little, there a little. (Isaiah 28:10)

Prayer

You have, O God, called and set apart some of Your servants to be teachers. We are grateful for those who are willing to be guardians and releasers of the mind. We thank You for those teachers who have shaped our own lives and pray that Norton Central High might become a place— no, might become a people—that will help form citizens who are informed, just, caring, curious, and growing.

Source of all truth, we thank You for those who exercise administration as a work of love. Bless them with discernment and patience and decisiveness. Show them Your example of power and place given up for service. And be with them in the lonely moments when they must make choices.

So, now we commission in Your name these to whom we entrust possibilities, that in all things we might serve You faithfully as we serve Your children effectively. Amen.

J O B

DECISION ABOUT QUITTING

Sometimes economics, morality, location, happiness, and/or family issues will lead persons to consider seeking new employment. It is not easy to let go of the known, even unpleasant circumstances, to risk income and opportunity in an unknown.

Example

For a time, Bob Berrino thought he had a dream job: travel, security, position, travel, advancement, travel, contacts, salary—did I mention travel? Finally, he had to make a decision whether or not to stay in this post that gave him everything except time for his family. Was it fair to make his family suffer financially? Was it right to exchange security for freedom? Was it a blot on his record to leave one company for another? What moral responsibility did he have to those who had employed him for thirteen years? He sat down with his pastor to "think out loud" about these things.

> *You shall eat the fruit of the labor of your hands;*
> *you shall be happy, and it shall go well with you. (Psalm 128:2)*

Prayer

Lord Jesus, how did you know when it was time to leave the carpenter's shop and begin your public ministry? Lord Jesus, how did you know when it was time to turn from traveling to teaching, from highways for healing to go instead toward Jerusalem, toward a cross? Lord Jesus, how do we know when it is time?

Your servant Bob bears now the burden of decision. Good values compete with good values. He opens himself—and we open ourselves with him—to the leading of Your Spirit to find his best place in serving You, in loving his family, and in being a faithful worker. Blow the wind of fresh wisdom upon him, and grant him such peace that he lives in the joy of knowing that nothing separates us from Your love in Christ Jesus, in Whose name we pray. Amen.

J O B

LOSS OF JOB

Both for reasons of self-esteem and self-preservation, many, if not most, persons find it important to contribute to family well-being and community life. Some do this with responsibilities at home; others seek public employment; some are self-employed. In any of these circumstances, it is disheartening to lose a job.

Example

Brenda Forsyth enjoyed her work at Wiggins Manufacturing; but when it was time to "tighten belts" at the company, she was surprised that she was suddenly unemployed. Brenda and Jack planned on having children after she worked for a couple more years: "long enough to get a little safety in the savings account." Her search for new employment was now a blend of anger, disappointment, sense of failure, loss of identity, and even desperation. She did not like to define herself as "out of work."

> God is our refuge and strength,
>   a very present help in trouble.
> Therefore we will not fear, though the earth should change,
>   though the mountains shake in the heart of the sea. (Psalm 46:1-2)

Prayer

It is true, Lord, that sometimes when we think we have found the key to life, the locks get changed. It hurts, O God; it hurts to be out of work. We name this before You not because we think You are absent from our concerns, but to affirm that we can come before You just as we are. And now Brenda comes: part of her dream unsettled, part of her self uncertain, part of her life uprooted. And she comes to You.

We pray for a spirit of healing, that Brenda might forgive any sense of unfairness that has shaped this day. We pray for a spirit of fullness, that Brenda might see her value in Your accepting love. We pray for a spirit at ease, that Brenda might present her best self to new employers.

Teach us the truth of reality as the place where You can meet us. Bless this hard time as a foothold for Your caring goodness, which we have seen in Jesus Christ our Lord. Amen.

JOB

LOOKING FOR WORK

A ny number of reasons can trigger a job search: newness to the work force, loss of previous job, dissatisfaction with present job, relocation, and/or need for greater income. Those seeking new employment sometimes feel like pieces of meat being examined at a meat market. It is not an easy time. Pastoral support is important.

Example

Armin Fischer just graduated from college, happily and expectantly equipped with a degree in history. What to do? Teaching? Human relations? Research? Sales? Management? Government service? The first few job interviews brought forth the classic statement: "Don't call us; we'll call you." Armin was disappointed and brought his apprehension to his pastor.

> Therefore do not worry, saying "What will we eat?" or "What will we drink?" or "What will we wear?" For it is the Gentiles who strive for all these things; and indeed your heavenly Father knows that you need all these things. But strive first for the kingdom of God and his righteousness, and all these things will be given to you as well. (Matthew 6:31-33)

Prayer

Gracious God, we have seen in Jesus Christ that the final word is a good one. We thank You. But we are not as sure about the words we hear for these days, words that sound more like no than yes, words that sound more like not now than of course, words that sound more like empty than full. Your servant Armin is ready to work but doors seem tight; doors seem locked; doors only creak.

Your promise is a presence and we claim it. Your presence is a promise and we claim it. We pray for a gift of patience that will grow to a gift of peace that will grow to a gift of place. Thank You for the final good word and for this day's blessing, which we receive through Jesus Christ our Lord. Amen.

J O B

RETIREMENT

Closing out a career of employment can be both renewing and frightening. In a society that often defines worth in terms of work, a person facing retirement finds a new sense of freedom as well as a new sense of self-evaluation.

Example

On the office desk of Emilio de Jesus was a reverse clock, counting down the days, hours, and minutes until retirement was official. Each evening when Turner Angles left for the late shift at Glosson Brothers, he glanced at a large wall calendar; his retirement date of August 15 was circled. Connie Mewborn looked again at the list posted on the employee bulletin board. Yes, her name was listed with those eligible for retirement. Pastor Mozart Gregory (I got the name because my parents wanted me to be a musician) suggested that Emilio, Turner, and Connie join him for some time to reflect on the impending retirements.

> *Let the favor of the Lord our God be upon us,*
> *and prosper for us the work of our hands—*
> *O prosper the work of our hands! (Psalm 90:17)*

Prayer

Lord Jesus, Who knew the work of a carpenter shop, You have been with these Your brothers and sister as they too have tasted the joy of accomplishment, the frustration of drudgery, the benefits of employment, and now the anticipation of retirement. Through all the changing scenes on life's stage, You have been the One Who brought meaning and purpose and direction. Now, in this particular time before retirement, we pray for days of fulfillment and years of growth.

When fears would rob us of faith, when emptiness would take the throne in our lives, when false busy-ness would prevent space meant for You, good Lord, deliver us.

Even as we thank You for years of work; of food, clothing, and shelter; of times to be re-created; we thank You for the times ahead, for victories in struggles not yet fought, and for the worth we find in being Your child.

In the name of the God Who created, and still creates; in the name of the God Who saved, and still saves; in the name of the God Who sustained us, and still sustains, we pray. Amen.

P E T S

DEATH

Pets mean a lot of different things to those who live with them: companionship, loyalty, responsibility, entertainment, recreation, beauty, and even a few negative things (messes, expense, more messes, burden). The death of a pet changes all that.

Example

James Otwell called his pastor: "I feel sort of silly mentioning this, but I just wanted to let you know. Remember how often I talked about my beagle Betsy? Well, she died this morning." James tried to keep his voice from breaking. "I got her when she was just a puppy fifteen years ago. I just wanted to let you know." Within thirty minutes, James' pastor knocked on his door.

> He gives to the animals their food,
> and to the young ravens when they cry. (Psalm 147:9)

Prayer

O God of all creation, You have created us for kinship, relationships with all the created order. We are grateful when Your creatures live together in harmony. We are thankful for the gifts You give us through friends with four legs. With the warmth of Betsy, You have given James the special presence of close bonds, both for days with clouds and for days with sun. With the dependency of Betsy, You have given James the wider understanding of love, of sharing, of caring.

Even as we thank You for these marks of mercy, we acknowledge the pain of separation. Grant now the award of happy recall. And bless us so to value the fullness of Your creation that we might seek to live in peace with air, water, and mineral, and to live in concord with the animals You give into our care. Help our hurts to heal, through the One who loved enough to seek one lost lamb, even Jesus Christ our Lord. Amen.

NEW PET

There is joy and anticipation as a new pet comes into the home. Who will care for it? Who will get to name it? Who will clean up after it? Where does it get to sleep? Who will take it to the vet?

Example

"A snake? You want a pet snake?" When Kira's mother promised her daughter a pet as a twelfth birthday present, she assumed that her daughter would pick a dog or a cat or maybe a goldfish. But now she stood with Kira at the counter of the pet store, ready to bring "Boomer" home in a special reptile carrier. "I'll take care of him; I promise," Kira said. Her mother took one more look at the newest member of the family, curled at the bottom of the cage, and said, "Welcome, Boomer."

Look at the birds of the air; they neither sow nor reap nor gather into barns, and yet your heavenly Father feeds them. (Matthew 6:26a, b)

Prayer

Not a sparrow falls, O God, without Your knowledge. And in Your wisdom, You have given us watch over all You have created. Thank You for giving us friends from Your creation. Grant us the ways to love them wisely and open us to learn from them. Teach us the patience we need to be good caregivers. Help us to connect even with this snake that we can come to marvel even more at the mystery of your life-giving grace.

Thank you for trusting us with new experiences. Give us a depth of affection sufficient to sustain our responsibilities when the days are not as good as this one. Give us some reflection of Your love for all of creation that we might be Your faithful stewards. And bless Boomer that any fright he feels might be tempered by our calm, and any strangeness he senses can become peace that we hold in common. Our prayer is in the name of Jesus Christ, the firstborn of all creation, through Whom all has been made. Amen.

P E T S

BIRTH

When a favorite pet gives birth, it can sometimes seem like an extension of one's own family. Waiting for puppies to be born, for example, can reflect some of the same anxiety, expectation, and wonder we have in anticipating a human birth.

Example

Onetta was thrilled. "We've got four new puppies," she told Pastor Bergland at the door following Sunday morning service. "And they look just like their mother!" "Is Agatha okay?" the pastor (glad that he remembered the name of Onetta's pet collie!). "Fine," Onetta replied. "One of the puppies died, but four of them are doing great."

> O sing to the LORD a new song;
> sing to the LORD, all the earth. (Psalm 96:1)

Prayer

In the presence of new beginnings, O God, we stand in awe. In awareness of Your creative power, we stand in mystery. In the company of maternal care, we stand in gratitude.

All the earth, all of Your creatures, join to praise You. Agatha nurtures now these puppies, even as You have given her gifts for nurture. Agatha feeds now these puppies, even as You have given her gifts for feeding. Agatha watches now over these puppies, even as You have given her gifts for caring. We marvel at this bounty of gifts, spread throughout Your creation.

We thank You for the joy that these new lives bring to this home. Bless Onetta as she supports the growth and development of these young ones. We acknowledge the sadness that one has not lived, but we know You heed all of Your creation.

Thank you for the miracle of birth, ever Your signal that life does go on, moving us with gladness toward Your full tomorrow, seen even now in Jesus Christ our Lord. Amen.

P E T S

DECISION ABOUT EUTHANASIA

One of the most difficult moments in caring for a pet comes when all evidence seems to point to days only of pain, illness out of the reach of cure, and life without quality of relationship. We hide the decisions to be made behind softer terms—"putting him to sleep," "relieving her of her misery"—but the struggle to decide is far from soft.

Example

Many times, the Reverend Ernesto Rivas helped members of his congregation face tough choices; now he looked at such a decision that he himself had to make. The veterinarian said there was no prospect of good recovery for Ruby, the pastoral family pet cat. Broken bones and swollen organs gave unremitting suffering to this beloved feline friend. Her body simply was overwhelmed by the shock and power of having been hit by a passing car. "She might stay alive," the vet said, "but her days will be hard."

> Teach me good judgment and knowledge,
> for I believe in your commandments. (Psalm 119:66)

Prayer

Thank You, dear God, for the good days we have had with Ruby, this child of Your creation. Thank You for the happiness she has brought us with affection, the challenge she has given us with independence, and the delight she has delivered with play and energy.

Now, Giver of grace, we face the reality that You have given us dominion over, and responsibility for, these creatures whom You told us to name. Help us to control our own desires and selfish hopes so we are able to choose wisely what to do now. Set us free from the fear of wrong decisions so we shall not become paralyzed into indecision. Mark this moment with grace so we might move from this hard place into a peace that passes understanding; through Jesus Christ our Lord. Amen.

B U S I N E S S

OPENING OF STORE

A new store sometimes means a positive expansion for a community, but it can also mean a threat to existing business owners. A grand opening is an occasion for presenting the best face possible to potential customers and an effort to fit into the region. In some areas, this means asking local clergy to pray at the opening.

Example

Sarah Lentz was not sure what she should do. The manager of the mega-store opening near the church where Ms. Lentz was pastor had called and asked: "Reverend, can you offer a prayer at our big opening next month? All the local officials will be there, and I want to make sure that the religious community is represented." Ms. Lentz knew that the establishment of the newcomer business upset some long-present storeowners; yet many people were thrilled that "we get our own Big Green Store."

> Her merchandise and her wages will be dedicated to the LORD; her profits will not be stored or hoarded, but her merchandise will supply abundant food and fine clothing for those who live in the presence of the LORD. (Isaiah 23:18)

Prayer

Eternal God, the Author of life, the Source of what is important, the Giver of every good and perfect gift, we pause in the midst of these busy moments to acknowledge Your presence, to claim Your promises, and to commit to Your purposes.

Many will pass through these doors, bringing hurting and hungry places in their lives; bless them. Many will come this way in times of special joy and celebration; bless them. Many will offer themselves for employment and service through this store; bless them.

Watch over this community that we might measure ourselves more by fuller caring than by bottom lines and that we might not forget those whose journey does not allow them easy access to all that is needed. We pray for those who manage this store that they may do so with wisdom beyond the wisdom of the world. We pray for those who work in this store that they may find fulfillment in these responsibilities. We pray for those who shop here that they might choose wisely as good stewards of resources You have given them. Amen.

B U S I N E S S

Closing of Store

Many factors go into a decision to close a store: economic, personal, demographic, and social. Shutting down a business is positive for some (Now I can enjoy retirement!), painful for others (Things aren't what they used to be), and often a mixture of both feelings.

Example

Lane's Grocery had been a presence on Main Street in Greenetown for sixty years. Mark Lane's father started the business and turned it over to his son with the hope that the thriving little store would always be a place where local friends could gather for conversation and convenience. Most of the small town stores had given way to larger competitors, and now Lane's was closing too. Mark asked his pastor to have a prayer before they locked the door the last time.

> We know that all things work together for good for those who love God, who are called according to his purpose. (Romans 8:28)

Prayer

Look into our hearts, O God, and see our sadness. Look into our memories, O God, and see our fullness. Look into our future, O God, and see our hopes. So much of life has passed through these doors, Gracious One, and so much of this town's heartbeat has been felt within these walls! Hear us now as each of us names, aloud or within, remembrance of special moments. (*Pause*) Hear us as we name, aloud or within, suppliers and delivery workers who have come to this place. (*Pause*) Hear us as we name, aloud or within, customers who have blessed those who were here at Lane's to help. (*Pause*) Hear us as we name, aloud or within, family ties that have sustained us. (*Pause*) Hear us as we name, aloud or within, those whose tomorrow becomes more clouded because this store will not be here. (*Pause*)

But most of all, O God, hear our prayer of thanksgiving: for the gift of good days, for the survival through hard days, for the promise of new days. Take this door, soon to be locked; and let it be a sign of bitterness left behind, disappointment overcome, and a decision well made. Already, we claim Your promise never to leave us, and we claim it through Jesus Christ our Lord. Amen.

Business

Relocation

From time to time, companies will relocate headquarters or manufacturing facilities or distribution centers. Sometimes these moves happen quite unexpectedly; other times the change occurs after months or years of rumor. In any case, communities are disrupted and lives face major adjustments.

Example

The headline in the morning paper told the story: "Snow-grip Moving Factory Operations to East Coast." Bob Marley had worked for Snow-grip Tires for almost twenty years. Now he faced the possibility of losing his job or having to move his family a thousand miles. "I can't get a decent job here," Bob lamented to the Reverend Mr. Barclay. "And if I go east with the company, what would we do about the special school that our son Logan needs?"

> Hear my cry, O God;
> listen to my prayer.
> From the end of the earth I call to you,
> when my heart is faint. (Psalm 61:1-2a)

Prayer

Unglued, O Lord: what we thought we had established has become unglued. And now we bring to You all the upset and confusion that runs through our lives. We struggle with feelings that we have been betrayed by those for whom we have worked. We wrestle with anxiety about how we shall provide for family, for daily living. We grapple with decisions of staying here where we are known or moving east where we know no one. And in the deepest part of the heart, we even face the demon of guilt: if only we had worked harder or done a better job, would this move even be discussed?

Unglued. All is unglued . . . except your steadfast love. Out of that love, pour patience into our being. Out of that love, bring discernment to our random mind. Out of that love, touch with healing all the hurting places of our lives and of this community. Creator God, as we face decisions about a far place, remind us that for You there are no near and far places; You are ever present. And we claim that presence in the name of the tri-une God, Father, Son, and Holy Spirit. Amen.

STRIKE

Few situations lead a community to choose sides quite as much as a labor-strike. Management leaders feel they have done all they can; worker leaders feel they have made more than their share of sacrifice. "No more!" becomes the cry of both. Common ground seems far away.

Example

Geoffrey Davis and Bette Wright attend the same church. One is a line worker at Norris Industries; the other is the Norris vice president for human relations. Separately, each has sought Pastor Carol Bailey, asking for "prayerful support" during the early days of a union strike at Norris. Ms. Bailey said, "Bette, I fear our prayer chain will be incomplete unless Geoff is present; Geoff, I fear our prayer chain will be incomplete until Bette is present." The air was strained, but they met together.

So faith by itself, if it has no works, is dead. (James 2:17)

Prayer

God of the elephant, one of us holds the leg and says an elephant is round; one of us holds the tail and says the elephant is thin; one of us touches the trunk and says an elephant is snake-like; one of us reaches the side and says the elephant is huge. You are the Creator of the elephant. You know the whole creature.

There is brokenness in our community because no one of us sees the whole elephant, but we pray for a spirit that will listen to one another until we can indeed hear all that is to be said. We pray for a spirit that will trust that what we hear from the other can be trusted, and we pray for a spirit that will be trustworthy in all that we say.

Clear our eyes for a greater vision of justice. Clear our ears for a clearer word of truth. Move us so that we outdo one another only in showing zeal for You. Keep us at peace, in Your peace, until hand joins hand across the table so that we can taste even now the banquet we have together in Your coming kingdom; through Christ our Lord. Amen.

B U S I N E S S

NEW CONTRACT

When employers and employees come to terms about income and benefits, there is sometimes residual division. Whether there has been a strike, pre-strike negotiations, or successful conversations, the lines can easily be drawn into "them" and "us." A new contract can be the occasion for a fresh start.

Example

"It is in the best interest of our company, its stockholders, and its employees that we have come to an agreement about worker compensation for the next three years. All of us can make our plans and our life decisions knowing that we are now working as a team in agreement, rather than as enemies at odds. We are grateful for the open cooperation of all who have been involved in moving to this good place."

> Do two walk together
> unless they have made an appointment? (Amos 3:3)

Prayer

How wonderful when brothers and sister can dwell together in unity! We praise You for that gift today, O God. You have created us in Your own image; You have created us for relationships to reflect that image. We celebrate before You this new beginning in the life of the company and thank You for those who have worked to make it so.

We confess that we have not always walked side by side, but now we rejoice in the new contract that allows us all to face in one direction. Forgive us when we have lost sight of one another and grant us the corrective lens of Your love. Watch over us so we do not mistake a first step for a completed journey.

So move among us, O God, that our lips and our lives speak justice. So move among us, O God, that our walk and our words speak righteousness. So move among us, O God, that our signs and our sounds speak mercy. And at the last, may all praise be given to You, our Creator, Sustainer, and Savior. Amen.

FAMILY

REUNIONS

Getting together as an extended family can be a time of memory and joy, but also a time tinged with tension and sadness. Family disagreements hidden by miles can reappear when all the parties are in one place. Who has embarrassed us? Who has done well? Who is not here (so we can talk about them)?

Example

The McArthur family had scattered across several states, but every other July they got together at the "old home place," a farmhouse in east Tennessee. Derik McArthur was the only ordained pastor in the family, so he got duty as unofficial family chaplain. "We want you to pray again at the family reunion," his cousins told him. Derik thought of his sister Fran who hated the reunion question: "Aren't you married yet?" He recalled the death of Uncle Edgar, killed when he tried to rob a convenience store. Derik knew that all would be thinking of Aunt Patrice, senior matriarch and too sick to come. He thought of his own children, the youngest in the family. And he knew that first cousin Jan would tease him: "Why don't you give up preaching and get a real job?"

For this is the message you have heard from the beginning, that we should love one another. (1 John 3:11)

Prayer

O God, our Father, from whom every family in heaven and earth takes its name, hear the prayer of Your people McArthur. We come before You with a mix of wholeness and brokenness, with a mix of closedness and openness, with a mix of getting it right and getting it wrong. We need again Your blessing of grace that we might move toward that perfection to which You invite us.

Death has broken into our house, O Lord, so loss and hurt and shock and sadness weave their way among us. Say to us again that nothing separates us from Your love for us in Christ Jesus! For new life on both sides of life's river, we give You thanks. For those who have crossed over and for those who have just begun the journey, we give You thanks.

Hear the names of those of the past whom we remember. (I invite you to call those names aloud.) Hear the names of those of special need whom we call before You now. (I invite you to give those names aloud now.) Hear the names of all those who gather here this day and receive them into Your care. (I invite you to call out your name and the names of those for whom you speak.)

And grant us tomorrow in Your grace. Amen.

F A M I L Y

TRAVELING

The family joys and pressures of living together can be amplified when the joys and pressures of traveling are added in. During "vacation season" or when a family is preparing for an extended trip, a pastor might well give prayer attention to such occasions.

Example

For years, Jeremiah and Jeanine Johnson had saved for "this one big family adventure." The retired couple invited their son and his wife, their daughter and her husband, and all four grandchildren (ages four to twelve) to join them on a cross-country driving trek. The rented van was jammed with people, luggage, and stuffed animals. "Why do we have to leave Garber at home?" lamented the six-year-old, already missing the fuzzy puppy not yet housebroken. "How about a prayer before we leave?" Jeremiah Johnson asked his pastor.

> Hold me up, that I may be safe
> and have regard for your statutes continually. (Psalm 119:117)

Prayer

Eternal God, Your maternal love watches over us, cares for us, and seeks to keep us safe. We pray that Your loving presence may be real for this family. As they move from places of familiarity to places of novelty and change, grant them the steady assurance of Your traveling mercies.

When joy erupts, grant them celebration. When newness appears, grant them openness. When pleasures smile, grant them contentment. When boredom lingers, grant them patience. When tensions simmer, grant them peace. When danger threatens, grant them assurance. When home beckons, grant them love.

We thank You that You have created us for one another. For Jeremiah and Jeanine, whose generous affection makes this trip possible, we give You thanks. For all who join in this travel, that dreams might live and that family might share, we give You thanks. For Your company on all of our life journeys, we give You thanks; through Jesus Christ, the eternal Mark of Your mercy. Amen.

F A M I L Y

SINGLES

O ur society struggles with the meaning of family: immediate family, extended family, single-parent families, separated families, blended families—and singles: how are singles to be seen as family?

Example

Pastor Francisco Villanueva looked out at the diverse group gathered in the church fellowship hall. On Sunday, he had simply said, "Anyone interested in starting a singles group in our church meet here at 7:30 Tuesday night." Before him stood seventy-year-old widows, just-out-of-college men, recently divorced persons, a couple of high school dropouts, and some people he had not seen before.

> But in your hearts sanctify Christ as Lord. Always be ready to make your defense to anyone who demands from you an accounting for the hope that is in you. (1 Peter 3:15)

Prayer

God of us all, we who are made one in our baptism come with thanksgiving for life: its possibilities, its relationships, its unfolding arenas for Your grace. We who have been shaped by all that we have met are grateful that ultimately we are shaped by the saving and restoring power of Jesus Christ.

When there are broken places in our journeys, we ask for healing. When there are open places in our hearts, we ask for fulfillment. When there are joys in our path, we ask for gratitude. When there is meaning in our walk, we ask for strength. When there is loneliness in our days, we ask for companionship. When there is happiness in our lives, we ask for the gift of sharing.

We dare, O God, to ask because You came to us in a solitary figure, our brother Jesus Christ. We dare, O God, to ask because You gave us our wholeness in offerings from the Spirit. So now we pray in the name of the triune God, in the very Family in whom we find life. Amen.

F A M I L Y

MISSING FAMILY MEMBER

Few occasions make us feel more helpless than when we realize that a family member is missing: a child kidnapped, a parent with Alzheimer's who has wandered off, a despondent spouse who did not return from work, a military son missing-in-action.

Example

Did someone take little Georgia? Did she get lost while chasing her pet dog? Did she fall into some unknown, abandoned well? What could have happened? No one knew. Hundreds of volunteers began slow walks throughout the neighborhood; but now, two full days later, still no one had a clue. Each trip by her room produced special pain, unlike the pain of birth, unlike the pain of growing up, even unlike the pain of death. It was a pain felt more as shadow than as darkness or light.

> I lift up my eyes to the hills—
>   from where will my help come?
> My help comes from the LORD,
>   who made heaven and earth. (Psalm 121:1-2)

Prayer

"Jesus loves me; this I know, for the Bible tells me so." Lord God, as minutes turn to hours and hours turn to days, our ache becomes deeper, our fright becomes stronger, our hopes become dimmer. We so much want to gather our arms around Georgia, to hold her in our embrace of love, but we cannot. Only in our hearts can we hug her now, but we seek the shielding reach of Your protection. Surround her with the defense of Your company. Keep her safe from harms that we cannot even name and remind her of her Friend Jesus, Who called children to Himself.

Move with those who walk the streets and woods, those who travel highways and side paths, and those who stay here "just in case." We honor Your name for sending those who make the searches. We seek Your comfort for those who find life's ordinary places far removed and wonder only, "Where is Georgia?"

Through our tears, through our anger, through our guilt, through our emptiness, we see a Shepherd who looks for His lost lamb. Thank You, Messiah Jesus, for crying with us, for waiting with us, for being with us. And keep that guardian watch for this lamb, Georgia, for it is in Your name that we pray, Amen.

F A M I L Y

GETTING ALONG

Someone remarked that most of us could be called saints as long as our families did not tell what they know. The family can be the center for fulfillment or for abuse. The family can be the locale for support or for disparagement. Many persons have tasted some of each of these circumstances.

Example

The Taylor family is like most families in Eagle Mount Church. They seem to get along with one another fairly well; but the stresses of parenthood, the uncertainties of teen years, and the slams of childhood make for a volatile mix of emotions, hopes, and disappointments. The Taylors have a family custom: every year on Joe and Jean's anniversary, the pastor is invited to come and have prayer with the family.

I have no greater joy than this, to hear that my children are walking in the truth. (3 John 4)

Prayer

"Peace be unto this house." That is our prayer, O God, the Parent of us all. You who called us to live with Your promises and to have lives of discipline and instruction, we thank You for giving us one another. For in giving us one another, You have expanded our horizons, troubled our selfish contentment, and shown us that the path to perfect freedom is in service to You.

"Peace be unto this house." That is our confession of need, O God, the Healer of division. Our best does not always get it done, and we open ourselves to the fullness of Your company. Forgive us when anger and impatience control our decisions. Forgive us when disrespect and disregard shape our actions.

"Peace be unto this house." We are grateful for these years of marriage and the expansion of that love into children. For Joe, for Jean, for Rachel, for Treva, and for Alex: we pray for the blessing of warmth shared, hope sustained, and potential made real. We claim it even now through Jesus Christ our Lord. Amen.

F A M I L Y

ABUSE

Domestic abuse. Sexual abuse. Elder abuse. Child abuse. Few pastoral situations will evoke as much intensity of hurt, confusion, self-doubt, accusation, and tragedy as allegations of abuse within the family. Guilt and denial and truth and victimization and memory and anger blur as family (and those beyond) try to sort out relationships now torn asunder.

Example

"I didn't know what to do, so when I saw the bruises I called you and I called the police." Pastor Terry Forsyth knew this was no ordinary pastoral setting. Harold Albright was vivid with rage: "I knew that Alice did not like having my mother here, but I never thought she would hit her!" Harold unfolded an account of how his wife said Harold's elderly mother had fallen from bed, but Harold's mother had whispered to him, "Alice hit me."

> You shall rise before the aged, and defer to the old; and you shall fear your God: I am the LORD. (*Leviticus 19:32*)

Prayer

"Our Father, who art in heaven, hallowed be Thy name." You have taught us to honor father and mother, and we say before You that there is special pain when we see their pain; there is special anger when we see their upset. Bring to Harold now the gift of righteous anger and balance it with the wisdom of holy discernment.

All we can offer to You now is a home of shattered trust. All we can give as a place to begin is accusation met with denial and the ways in which there is inward and outward pain.

Watch over Your bruised servant. Give her a healing sense of Your presence. And give us Your hand to hold as we walk through this forest of division. Bless Harold and bless Alice that these difficult days ahead may be a journey to truth and peace, until finally the right thing is done and Your name is glorified; through Jesus Christ our Lord. Amen.

F A M I L Y

VICTIM OF ABUSE

Whether the recall is recent or a long-stored account, a person who has been a victim of verbal, emotional, physical, or sexual abuse in the home bears the marks of that violation. "Did it happen? Did I cause it? Did I deserve it? Should I report it? Can I trust my pastor? Can I trust myself? Whom can I trust?"

Example

"Are you sure?" Pastor Stillman knew that was not the right question to ask, but it was the only thing he could think of to say when Jason Livingston told him, "My daddy sexually molested me from the time I was six until I was sixteen." Jason's father, a long-time leader at St. Bartholomew Church, had died two years earlier. "I hope he is burning in hell!" exclaimed Jason. "No, I don't," he added, "because I want to ask him why he destroyed my life."

So it is not the will of your Father in heaven that one of these little ones should be lost. (Matthew 18:14)

Prayer

O God, Who hears the prayers of the lonely and the broken, hear our prayer of thanksgiving for the courage You have given Jason to face a memory, which even now haunts and harms. Thank You for the strength we claim for Jason as he moves toward hard choices of whom to tell, of what to do, of how to remember.

And we name before You Jason's father, one who gave public honor to Your name even as secret places shamed his heart and tormented his son. Perhaps it is too early to forgive, O God; perhaps it is too early to understand, O God; but we accept this as a time of beginning, of daring, and of opening the past.

Grant Jason the power of his worth given in his baptism. Begin to take away the crust that has bound him and wash him anew with healing waters. As Your Son has taught us to pray, "Deliver us from evil." Amen.

FAMILY

DENIAL OF ABUSE

W hen accused of domestic violence or some other form of family abuse, persons often deny the allegation or offer some explanation that makes sense to them. Sometimes they are right. Often they are wrong.

Example

Pam did not want to give her last name when she knocked on the parsonage door late at night. "I've got to have a place to hide. My husband keeps on beating me." The Reverend Ms. Drake helped Pam get to the care of a shelter. A few weeks later when Pam decided to try again to live with her husband, she asked Ms. Drake to go with her. "I love Pam," her husband said. "I welcome her home. I am a Christian man. I would never hit her. Never! It hurts me that she has made up these stories to get some attention. Why doesn't anybody listen to my side of the story? Why won't anybody believe I never hit her?"

> *They show that what the law requires is written on their hearts, to which their own conscience also bears witness; and their conflicting thoughts will accuse or perhaps excuse them on the day when, according to my gospel, God, through Jesus Christ, will judge the secret thoughts of all. (Romans 2:15-16)*

Prayer

Pam and Anthony are both Your children, O God, and now in differing ways each is hurting. This home is a fragile place and needs You to guard Your children as they try to walk amid the shards of glass of shattered trust. Echoes of accusation and denial drown out the sound of Your voice.

Your Word tells us that we are all sinners. Help us to find the sin that breaks us from You and separates us from one another. You have called us to an abundant life and have no desire for Your children to give or to receive abuse. Protect us from false understandings of ourselves and grant us grace that will survive those who for whatever reason bring us damage. Our anger comes from our fear, fear of retribution, fear of continued abuse, or fear of continued false accusation. Plant the seed of truth that Perfect Love might cast out that fear; through the cross-shaped gift of Christ's love. Amen.

FAMILY

CONFESSION OF ABUSE

The convicting power of God's grace can lead an abuser to confess and seek forgiveness. Confronted with evidence of the turmoil and trial that abuse has generated, an abuser may admit guilt and responsibility.

Example

Pastor David Hardin had not expected this phone call. His lay leader, Paula Lawson, said, "Pastor, I must see you immediately. I am heavily burdened." As they met, the reason for Ms. Lawson's distress became clear: "My daughter, Vanessa, called me last night and said social service was taking her three children away and putting them into foster care. It's my fault. I did cruel things to punish Vanessa when she was a little girl, and now she is doing those same things to her children. My sin is still devastating her life."

> But if we walk in the light as he himself is in the light, we have fellowship with one another, and the blood of Jesus his Son cleanses us from all sin. (1 John 1:7)

Prayer

It won't go away, Lord. Paula's pain won't go away. The wreckage she brought into the life of little Vanessa now visits another generation. It won't go away.

Hear this confession of sin. Listen to the heart of this penitent believer. (Paula: when the words I speak are the words of your heart, speak them after me.) I have sinned against You, O God. (*Pause*) I have abused Your child, Vanessa. (*Pause*) You gave Vanessa into my care, and I have failed both You and her. (*Pause*) Out of Your healing goodness, forgive me. (*Pause*) Out of Your power to create, make me a new creature. (*Pause*) Give me courage to confess this evil to Vanessa. (*Pause*) Give me opportunity to work for the good of my grandchildren. (*Pause*) Clear my being of hidden fault. (*Pause*) Through Jesus Christ, Who Himself said, "Father, forgive . . ." (*Pause*) Amen.

C H I L D R E N

BIRTH OF CHILD WITH SEVERE DISABILITY

After the anxious and varying feelings of anticipation during pregnancy, a couple faces new dimensions in their life when the newborn baby has severe disabilities. Sometimes these special circumstances are foreseen; sometimes no one expects such an eventuality.

Example

Pastor Tim Deer went to Mountain Hospital, ready to rejoice with Branson and Yvonne Harjo at the birth of their first child. The looks on the faces in the room sent him a quick signal: something is amiss. The doctors have told the Harjos that there can be little possibility for a normal quality of life for this baby. Uncertainty, anger, guilt, and fear push to take the place of joy, newness, plans, and hopes.

Then the LORD God formed man from the dust of the ground, and breathed into his nostrils the breath of life; and the man became a living being. (Genesis 2:7)

Prayer

Creator God, the mysteries of life are within Your hand. This place of birth now carries with it both the thanksgiving for parents who have awaited this gift and the uncertainty of days that now unfold in unexpected ways. We are grateful that Yvonne has borne well the season of pregnancy and the stresses of delivery. We thank You that new life and new responsibilities and new tomorrows have been given to the Harjo family.

Your Son asked that children be brought to Him in order that He might bless them. Your Son said that all of us must become as children if we hope to enter the kingdom of heaven. So we bring this baby to be blessed by Jesus. And we open ourselves to learn from this child, that we might be ready for Your kingdom.

Touch our disappointments with new ways of being. Hear our angers with assurances of grace. Relieve our guilt with the balm of Gilead. And restore the joy of birth: relationships in which all can grow, opportunities not yet revealed, and the gracious stewardship of a life. You have trusted us with one of Your own, and we are grateful; through Jesus Christ, the Word become flesh, we pray. Amen.

CHILDREN

ADOPTION

Children change things! When persons adopt a baby, a young boy, a young girl, or perhaps a teenager, they are choosing a future that will be different. And the choice of adoption has made life different for the one being received into the home.

Example

Three faces seemed to have especially big smiles, as the door of 4233 Repton Street swung open. Two of those faces belonged to the adults who had said yes to parenthood; one face belonged to a six-year-old girl, moving now into a home she could call her own. "We are really here," Jennifer said as she hugged each one, including the man she said was now "my pastor."

> Let your work be manifest to your servants,
> and your glorious power to their children. (Psalm 90:16)

Prayer

"Praise God from whom all blessings flow!" What joy, what abundant joy, fills this home today! What bounty, what rich bounty, abides in each heart! For now one plus one equals three! We are grateful for the love that invites Jennifer into this family. We are grateful for the love that Jennifer brings to this family.

You showed us in Jesus how much You love children. Help us all to reflect the love of Jesus. You showed us in Jesus how much You want us to care for one another. Help us all reflect the caring of Jesus. You showed us in Jesus how You enjoy giving us new beginnings. Help us all reflect the new creation of Jesus.

Today, for this home, You have spelled happiness "J-e-n-n-i-f-e-r." Thank You and give her parents wisdom and patience and hearing and hopefulness. Thank You and give Jennifer energy and growth and learning and peacefulness.

And give us all the closer companionship of our Lord Jesus Christ, in Whose name we pray. Amen.

CHILDREN

CUSTODY

When parents separate, thorny decisions have to be made about the custody of children. Although these arrangements can be made without acrimony, the plans are sometimes fraught with resentment and a sense that the children have become pawns in the parental fight. It is hard to determine "the best interests of the child."

Example

Evan dreaded going to visit his mother. It was not so much that he did not enjoy being with her, but simply being at her apartment would remind him in so many ways that she and his father had gone separate ways. Each parent tried hard not to speak ill of the other, but Evan was left to wonder: Who is to blame? Is it my fault? Can they get back together? Will my friends still like me? Those are tough questions for an eleven-year-old.

He will turn the hearts of parents to their children and the hearts of children to their parents. (Malachi 4:6a)

Prayer

Lord, tonight Evan and I want to talk with You. We know that You go with Your people when they have to travel on hard journeys. And right now, Evan is on a hard journey. He loves his mother, and he loves his father, and he is sad that they do not love each other. His mother loves him, and his father loves him, and he is glad that they still care for him. We tell You this, Lord, not because we think You do not know already, but because You have told us to pour out our hearts before You, and this is what is on our hearts.

Thank You for the freedom You give Evan to have strong feelings: sometimes love, sometimes anger, sometimes confusion, sometimes guilt, sometimes loneliness, sometimes happiness. Even though we have "sometimes" feelings, we are glad that You are an "all the time" God. Stay with Evan so he is never alone. Go with Evan so he can walk with courage. Be with Evan as surely as Jesus told the children to come to Him.

We ask this so Evan can continue to grow to become fully the young man You would have him be: Your child, loved and accepted, marked by his baptism in the name of the Father, the Son, and the Holy Spirit. Amen.

Civic

BLESSING OF A MEETING

Even in a society that separates church and state, there is often a request for a prayer before civic occasions. Aware of the range of religious journeys present, the one who prays seeks to be faithful to his or her own discipleship while acknowledging that not everyone has experienced God in the same way.

Example

The chairperson of the State Association of Graphic Artists knew that one of their former members, Brenda McCauley, was now in seminary. "Brenda, how about saying a little prayer at the start of the Association banquet next week?" Brenda grimaced at the casual attitude toward prayer, but decided to accept the invitation.

> *They asked, and he brought quails,*
> *and gave them food from heaven in abundance. (Psalm 105:40)*

Prayer

Creator God, the Giver of life, the Source of strength, and the Hope of our tomorrows, we thank You for the possibilities within this Association. You have given us friends and colleagues, and we are grateful. Move our gratitude to become compassion for the friendless and companionship for the lonely.

You have given us meaningful work, and we are grateful. Move our gratitude to become generosity toward those who are empty and patience with those who are without purpose. You have given us a bounty of food, and we are grateful. Move our gratitude to become outreach to the hungry and energy for greater service.

We offer our art to You, not to earn Your favor but to honor Your presence. We offer ourselves to You, not to claim goodness but to say thank you. And that is our word for this time: thank You. Amen.

Civic

Political Event

Partisan political events may seem like strange places for prayer. Although God surely cares deeply about important decisions in political life, there is hubris and arrogance in identifying that caring with our political divisions.

Example

"Dr. Martin-Worthy, the planning committee wants to have an invocation at the start of our state party convention. Because you are my pastor, I wanted to ask you to give that prayer." Hesitating, Dr. Martin-Worthy finally spoke with a nervous laugh: "I'll ask God's blessing, but I don't think I want to tell God how to vote!"

> He said to them, "Then give to the emperor the things that are the emperor's, and to God the things that are God's." (Luke 20:25)

Prayer

God of all the nations, You have called all people to lives of righteousness and justice. You have called all people to lives of peace and wholeness. But we confess that sometimes we have cared more for lofty places than we have for places of service. We confess that sometimes we have worked more for power than we have for purpose.

Bless now those who gather in this place. Give the gifts of discernment. Give the gifts of wisdom. Give the gifts of vision. To those who lead here, grant the patience of cooperation. To those who debate here, grant clarity of thought. To those who decide here, grant the courage for truth.

Keep ever before us the broken places of our life together, places of despair and disappointment. Set our ears to hear the cry of the poor. Set our eyes to see the needs of the sick. Set our hearts to beat in rhythm with Yours. And blend us with all people of good will, both in this place and beyond, in order that this state might be a signal of hope and fulfillment. Amen.

CIVIC

MEAL BLESSING

For all kinds of public events, pastors offer a blessing before a meal. Most pastors will be aware of who will be present and will seek to pray in such a way that the prayer can be one on behalf of all those gathered.

Example

Each year, Silvertown civic clubs come together to have a "Community Thank You" banquet for fire fighters, police personnel, and emergency medical technicians. Persons representing every dimension of the region enjoy the meal and the chance to express appreciation for those who protect and serve them. The invitation to offer the opening prayer always goes to the newest pastor in town.

I appeal to you therefore, brothers and sisters, by the mercies of God, to present your bodies as a living sacrifice, holy and acceptable to God, which is your spiritual worship. (Romans 12:1)

Prayer

You have created us for life in community, O God, and we are grateful for those relationships that sustain and support our life together. We thank You for those women and men who serve us with the protection, care, and security You want to give to all Your children.

Now before us are plates of Your bounty. Bless this food. Bless those whose labor stirred in unseen fields in order that we might eat. Bless those whose skills have brought to us the crops that now feed us. Bless those whose hands of preparation have chopped and mixed and blended and cooked in order that these gifts might be pleasing to our palates. Bless those who move among us in service in order that our meal might be a time of relaxation and renewal. Bless those in other places who are hungry, even as we are nourished.

In thanksgiving for those who serve You in these public duties, in thanksgiving for a Silvertown that cares, in thanksgiving for this meal, we give You praise. We give You praise. Amen.

C I V I C

INSTALLATION OF PUBLIC OFFICIALS

Either because of the request of an elected official or because of long-standing tradition, ceremonies of inauguration or installation often include a prayer. Pastors need to remember that when there have been election winners, there have also been election losers.

Example

When Dal Joon Yang became pastor at St. James Church, he did not know that he was becoming the pastor of a woman soon to be elected mayor of Macon City. Shortly after the election results were announced, Mayor-elect Alexander called her pastor and asked, "Will you offer a prayer as part of the program when I become the mayor?" The Reverend Mr. Yang knew that the voting had been close and bitterly contested.

Moreover, it is required of stewards that they be found trustworthy.
(1 Corinthians 4:2)

Prayer

Eternal God, Who has sought Your people across the generations, we open ourselves to Your presence in this moment of newness for our city. We are grateful for the freedom in which we have been able to choose a leader. We are thankful for all those who offered themselves for this place of service and vision. We are glad to praise You on this day which stirs hope for some, which brings disappointment for some, but which is a time for acknowledging Your goodness by all.

Now, we pray for Louise Alexander. Move her to faithful stewardship of this post. Protect her from putting self above people. Grant her a sensitive heart, a clear mind, a willing spirit, and an active courage. And bless this city she will lead. Grant us the gifts to be a place of peace and the generosity to be a people of welcome. Give us a special love for those who seem left out by virtue of loneliness and hunger and despair.

In Your name, we commission Mayor Alexander for this place of trust and responsibility. Set her feet in this good office that she might serve wisely with both caution and risk, and always to Your glory. Amen.

C I V I C

FUND-RAISER

Most communities experience a series of efforts to raise money for a variety of good causes. There are kick-off banquets, meetings for updates, challenges for the workers, and closing celebrations. These are often seen as an occasion for prayer.

Example

The Foundation for Community Care was established some years ago to raise funds to build a regional health center for the remote village of Willow. This year, in addition to trying to generate money locally, the directors of the Foundation decided to seek gifts in the nearest cities, almost two hours away. "Pray for us, pastor," the request came to the Reverend Mr. Sharpe along with an invitation to the planning meeting.

> The LORD is my light and my salvation;
>   whom shall I fear?
> The LORD is the stronghold of my life;
>   of whom shall I be afraid? (Psalm 27:1)

Prayer

After each petition, I shall invite you to respond: "Holy God, hear our prayer."

In Your presence, always in Your presence, O God, we gather and ask You to receive our prayer of praise, our word of thanksgiving, our expression of hope. And Your people say: "Holy God, hear our prayer."

In Your promise, always in Your promise, O God, we see a day to come when all Your family in Willow will find a home for healing and a haven for health. And Your people say: "Holy God, hear our prayer."

In Your plenty, always in Your plenty, O God, we seek to release those funds that will move us even closer to making Willow a community of wholeness. You go before us into these efforts and we are grateful. And Your people say: "Holy God, hear our prayer." Amen.

CIVIC

DEDICATION OF PUBLIC BUILDING

U sually, a community is proud of new infrastructure, new facilities, and new public buildings. Occasionally, however, these occurrences are marked by bitter public discourse. Praying in that tension can be a challenge!

Example

When the Town of Hendrix completed its first public water plant, most of the residents rejoiced that safe, plentiful water would be available throughout the community. Others, however, had protested the tax increase and had argued that the environment was being harmed. Jimmy Dell was pastor at Hendrix Memorial Church, the oldest and largest congregation in the small town. No one was surprised when Pastor Dell stood to offer prayer at the opening of the water plant.

> *The LORD will guide you continually,*
> *and satisfy your needs in parched places,*
> *and make your bones strong;*
> *and you shall be like a watered garden,*
> *like a spring of water,*
> *whose waters never fail. (Isaiah 58:11)*

Prayer

Eternal God, the Fountain of Life, Whose love is an ever-flowing stream, we have gathered on a day important to our town and now seek the refreshment of Your Spirit. Bless us with grace that we might live together in goodness. Bless the fruit of our common decision-making. And bless those now served by this supply of water.

For those who will be enlivened by this water, we give You thanks. For those children, who will, with protest, enter into clean bath water, we give You thanks. For those homes where daily chores and daily life will move more easily, we give You thanks. For those who will refresh tired flowers, we give You thanks. For those who will laugh as they run through lawn sprinklers, we give You thanks. For those whose labor will be enabled by the revival of water, we give You thanks.

Bless with safety those who work in this place. Bless with patience those who are uncertain about this place. Bless with joy those who find this day, this place, to be a good day, a good place, for Hendrix. And together, all Your people say: Amen.

HOLIDAYS

MARTIN LUTHER KING JR. DAY

This newest of United States official holidays honors the vision and courage of Dr. King. The day becomes a time of "taking the civil rights temperature" of this country. Community events, when developed widely, bring together a cross section of people, reclaiming "the dream."

Example

The Reverend Michael Bickerton Jr. was pleased to be invited to give a prayer at the start of the MLK Day parade. Several thousand people lined the streets of the city, some simply to enjoy the bands and floats, some excited about the marchers, some reminiscing about days of protest, some wanting to pass on a legacy to a new generation, some glad to have a day off from school, some committed to justice and human rights, some in prayerful gratitude for Dr. King.

> But let justice roll down like waters,
> and righteousness like an ever-flowing stream. (Amos 5:24)

Prayer

God of justice and peace and power, You raise up servants to proclaim Your truth. You send prophets to be Your messengers. You make uncomfortable claims upon us by putting into our midst those who live out the demands of love. We thank You for Your servant Martin, Your prophet Martin, Your love-demanding Martin.

Too often we have turned from Your will and sought only our own place at the table. Remind us of a vision in which all Your children gather to eat. Too often we have closed our ears to challenges to change. Remind us of a word that asks not "what is easy" but "what is right." Too often we have settled for "this is good enough." Remind us of a call to live a dream for all of Your children, whatever hue, whatever language, whatever place.

We know, O God, that Martin walked in his own imperfect way to follow One who walked a perfect way. You led Martin on his journey, and we pray that You lead us now. Amen.

H O L I D A Y S

EASTER

At the core of the gospel message is the resurrection of Jesus Christ. Easter traditions, some of them secular in origin, fill up family time. Church services burst with energy and celebration. Christ is alive!

Example

At first, Wesley Perkins was bothered that he could think of nothing new to say on Easter Sunday. Then he realized that his problem was something to be celebrated: the fact that the news of this Easter is exactly the same news of the first Easter! He is risen! He is risen indeed! On Easter Sunday afternoon, the parsonage phone rang. "Pastor Perkins, this is Bernice Gilbert. I am sorry to bother you, but I need your prayers. All day today everyone has seemed so joyful, but I can only feel sadness. It is the first Easter after Gil died. Can you pray with me over the phone?"

Jesus said to her, "I am the resurrection and the life. Those who believe in me, even though they die, will live." (John 11:25)

Prayer

God of the morning, sometimes we find ourselves at night. The evening fog rolls through our hearts and minds, waiting for daybreak. In Your Son, Jesus Christ, the warmth of the sunlight has burst from the tomb and begun to burn away the fog, until the daylight can be seen again.

Our prayer now is for Bernice. In the midst of the Easter happiness all around her, she feels lonely. Receive that loneliness as the only gift she can bring to You now. Accept her memories of Gil as an offering. Generous God, You are able to take what we bring in earthen vessels and turn it into treasure.

God of new life, even life beyond death, bring the victory of Easter even when we miss the joy. God of new hope, even hope beyond this moment, bring the gift of Easter even when we still wait outside the tomb. We pray in the name and presence of the risen Christ, our Lord and our Savior. Amen.

LABOR DAY

For almost one hundred twenty-five years, the United States has set aside a day to recognize working people. The holiday is a strange blend of civic, religious, economic, sociological, and shopping (!) virtues.

Example

On the Sunday nearest Labor Day, Pastor Svetlana Matveyeva invited her parishioners to wear their working clothes to the service of worship at First Church. What a mixture! Nurse uniforms were next to three-piece suits. Butcher apron sat side by side with attire marked "Southside Auto Repair." One woman threw a diaper over her shoulder! There were: student sweaters, coach's sweatpants (complete with whistle), artist's smock, and Ms. Matveyeva's clerical collar.

> *People go out to their work*
> *and to their labor until the evening. (Psalm 104:23)*

Prayer

Creating God, Who made us for each other, we thank You for placing in us skills, talents, strengths, energies, and learnings that we may offer for the common good. We are appreciative of the range of life You have called together in this congregation. On this time near Labor Day, hear our gratitude for those who work in unseen places. Hear our thanks for those who undertake the unpleasant tasks that make days more pleasant for others. Hear our gratitude for those who work in places of high duty and responsibility.

Our thanksgiving must be blended with our confession, O God, for we have too easily taken for granted work done by others. We have too quickly given more value to some labor than to others. And we have too often forgotten those who have no job, who have no employment, not by choice, but by circumstance.

In Your Holy Word, we see Your presence in work: Nehemiah building a wall, Ruth and Boaz gathering crops, the hammering and sawing of our Lord in the carpenter shop, the tent-making of the apostle Paul, and the generosity of Lydia, the seller of goods made with expensive purple. Thank You for blessing work. We pray for Your protective arms around those who sweat in dangerous places, Your gentle comfort for those who toil in drudgery, and Your fulfilling grace for those whose labor has lost meaning. Create in us clean hearts, O God, that our places of occupations might become places of mutual benefit; through Jesus Christ our Lord. Amen.

H O L I D A Y S

COLUMBUS DAY

When some persons hear a claim that Columbus discovered America in 1492, they wonder: How could he "discover" a place where native people already lived? There is a tension between the gain of values brought by some of the Europeans who moved here and the sidetracking of values by which Native Americans had lived here.

Example

The local radio station wanted to celebrate Columbus Day and invited the Reverend Dwayne Reggio to give a prayer as the holiday began. Mr. Reggio knew that for some traditions, Columbus Day was not a time of celebration, but was an occasion of somber reflection on loss and on "what might have been." He accepted the invitation.

> "And the LORD said, 'What have you done? Listen; your brother's blood is crying out to me from the ground!'" (Genesis 4:10)

Prayer

Loving God, You have made all people of one blood. You have created us to be one people with a variety of gifts, and when we deny or destroy the gifts of others, we deny or turn away from part of Your creation. Forgive us when we make ourselves the standard by which right and wrong are measured, when we make ourselves the criterion by which good and bad are tested.

On this day, we are grateful that You have planted within us energy for exploration and openness to Your broader world. We remember Christopher Columbus who lived out those blessings. Yet, there have been times on these shores when the opportunity of blessing became the occasion for brokenness. God of us all, forgive us.

Now teach us new duties for living together. Teach us that brother is brother and sister is sister and that our family is never as strong as when we are family as one. When the sins of those before us continue to visit us, grant us a handle for picking up our possibilities.

All of this we ask because Your love is sufficient and we want our love to bring You glory. So be it. Amen.

Holidays

Thanksgiving

The beginnings of this holiday are shrouded in the mists of history, but many people in the United States see Thanksgiving growing out of gratitude for survival. Sometimes Native Americans have painful recall of the violation of their land. Families often come together for a meal, rich in both calories and tradition.

Example

Thanksgiving at the Lopez house is going to be filled with family, food, and football, all three a part of how they enjoy this holiday's extra long weekend. There is special joy because Grandpa Lopez and Tía María are bouncing back from illness and will be present. Oscar is bringing his girlfriend, Alicia, to meet the family. As Mrs. Lopez stirred the secret ingredient into her homemade dessert, she wondered aloud: "How can any one family be so blessed! What a wonderful Thanksgiving!"

> [G]iving thanks to God the Father at all times and for everything in the name of our Lord Jesus Christ. (Ephesians 5:20)

Prayer

"O God, our help in ages past, our hope for years to come, our shelter from the stormy blast, and our eternal home!" You have indeed, O God, been with this family across the generations, in ages past. You do love us in such a way, Holy One, that we dare to have anticipation of love tomorrow, hope for years to come. You have watched over us during illness and separations, a shelter of grace. You have promised us the full gift of life, an eternal home.

We make our prayer of thanksgiving for better health for Grandpa Lopez and for Tía María; we make our prayer of thanksgiving for love that blossoms for Oscar and Alicia; we make our prayer of thanksgiving for all the family gathered here, not only under one roof, but under one Lord.

This food is a reminder of how fully You have blessed us in the past year, so in giving You thanks for this food, we thank You for all Your abundance. Keep our hearts aware of those who bear these days in pain and hunger so we may become instruments of Your plenty. Hear us as we pray as the Lord Jesus taught us, "Our Father . . . "

CHRISTMAS

Whether it is a family meal or an early morning time at the Christmas tree or a traditional gathering of extended kin, the Yuletide season brings an interesting blend of joy and tiredness and memory and hope.

Example

Trent Jackson remembered how the family of his childhood had begun every Christmas morning: the children gathered in the hallway, Dad read the Christmas story from Luke, and Mom said a prayer. Then the family brought eager smiles into the living room for the laughing and loving exchange of gifts. This year, it was up to Trent to offer the prayer with his children, young ones who paced anxiously in the hallway.

And she gave birth to her firstborn son and wrapped him in bands of cloth, and laid him in a manger, because there was no place for them in the inn. (Luke 2:7)

Prayer

"Glory to God in the highest heaven, and on earth peace among those whom he favors!" We thank You, O God, for the gift of Jesus, from Whom we have learned how to give. We thank You, O God, for the love of Jesus, from Whom we have learned how to love. We thank You, O God, for the serving strength of Jesus, from Whom we have learned how to be strong by serving.

We remember those now gone who in times past have gathered with us on Christmas morning; now they praise You at Your eternal throne. We think of those who are as close as our hearts but who are miles away; now they praise You in a oneness with us that is not defined by distance. We gather as a family this morning with gratitude for each one here; now we praise You with the excitement this day brings.

Hear us as we name our special joys of this day. (Members of the family state these joys aloud.) Hear us as we name those for whom this is not a happy day: the poor, the lonely, the brokenhearted, the rich who have found life empty, the families who have vacant places at today's table. In silence, we pray for them. (Here there is a period of silent reflection.)

Now, remembering that all good things come from You, O Lord, we offer this Christmas celebration as our way of enjoying the birth of our Savior, even Jesus Christ. Amen.

Holidays
New Year

R eligious services, family parties, late-night television, well-intended resolutions, Watch Night, toasts and treats: any or all of these (plus going to bed early!) might well make up the new year's observance.

Example

Pastor Barker was invited to the Creighton Heights neighborhood New Year's Eve party, but there was one unusual stipulation: "At midnight, we want you to offer a prayer." The occasion was not one at which the pastor felt comfortable; there was much drinking and boisterous partying. But indeed just before midnight, the host sought out Frank Barker. "I'll get them quiet and you have the prayer. It's something we always do at these parties." Pastor Barker wondered how others had prayed at this raucous event.

> The steadfast love of the LORD never ceases,
>   his mercies never come to an end;
> they are new every morning;
>   great is your faithfulness. (Lamentations 3:22-23)

Prayer

O God, Who reads our hearts before we speak our words, we stand on the cliff of a new year. The view from this height is gorgeous with possibilities, but the dangers at this height are many. The year comes with more questions than answers, but we declare one gift of sureness: Your love.

Forgive us for the ways in which we have turned aside from Your love or have pretended that it was only for those whom we loved. Forgive us for the casualness with which we treat sacred relationships. Forgive us for the way in which we measure life by self and not by service.

O God of new creation, move us toward new beginnings. In this moment of silence, hear the promise of each heart for the new year. (*Silence*) When we fail to bring our best, remind us of the promise here made, and with the brightness of Your light, shine upon the paths of the days ahead. Great is Your faithfulness. Amen.

E L D E R L Y

VOLUNTARILY GIVING UP DRIVING

In most regions of the United States, the use of the automobile is a sign of valued independence and full mobility. To give up driving often creates a sense of despair and emptiness. Some persons give up driving in their later years.

Example

Although most elderly drivers have better driving records than younger persons, Yvonne Locklear no longer felt safe driving on the crowded streets of Los Angeles or on the busy interstate highways surrounding the city. Finally, at age 87 she turned in her driver's license. Daughter Jeanine had encouraged her mother to take this step "before something happens." In her characteristic positive spirit, Mrs. Locklear gave a bittersweet party to celebrate "all my years of freedom." Was freedom now a thing of the past?

"All things are lawful for me," but not all things are beneficial. "All things are lawful for me," but I will not be dominated by anything. (1 Corinthians 6:12)

Prayer

O God of vigilant care, You have given such good life to your servant Yvonne Locklear: joy in living, family of loving, and seventy years behind the wheel! We give You thanks.

Hear us as we name some good moments of memory as Yvonne has driven. (Here, those present are invited to recall trips together, unusual car experiences with Yvonne, even funny things that happened on travels.)

Our prayer is one of thankful memory. Now, as Yvonne accepts the wisdom of her caution and releases responsibility and opportunity for transportation to others, grant grace and patience sufficient for these days of transition. Even as we confess anxiety about what it can be like to be without car at beck and call, we thank You for the perfect freedom that is found in Christ Jesus.

We give You thanks for the courage with which Yvonne has made her decision. In Your covenant of care, we commit ourselves to support her. Come with peace into all the changing places of life. Come with joy, which will fill our tomorrows; through our blessed Messiah, Your Son, our Savior, even Jesus our Lord. Amen.

ELDERLY

INVOLUNTARILY GIVING UP DRIVING

Anger, disappointment, and a sense of betrayal may erupt when someone is told he or she may no longer drive. When the driver is elderly or frail, this loss of independence may appear to be yet another loss of dignity, pride, and function.

Example

"Mama," Joy Charleston said to her mother, "We have talked about this before, but it is time to do something. I need to keep the keys to your car before you hurt yourself or someone else." Barbara Charleston's eyes brimmed with tears and with fury. "You just want my car! Why don't you just steal it! All of this because I made one mistake at the mall parking lot!" "Mama, that was the fourth time you backed into another car. I'm worried about you. I love you." "You sure have a funny way of showing it!" her mother screamed back.

Honor your father and your mother, so that your days may be long in the land that the LORD *your God is giving you. (Exodus 20:12)*

Prayer

Lord God, You have taught us to come to You in the times of our deepest valleys. We know that nothing separates us from Your love seen in Christ Jesus. So now we bring the hurt and confusion and despair that Barbara feels as she faces a new stage of her journey.

Your protective care comes in many ways: sometimes our own good judgment, sometimes the voice of a hidden conscience, sometimes the acts of those who love us, sometimes the miracle of Your unseen presence. But we have to admit, O God, that when tomorrow is shaped like a question mark, we are not always sure about today. Sometimes we need for You to paint Your love in bright colors.

Holy One, this transition is not really about driving; it is about freedom, independence, and self-worth. These are no small matters, so our pain is very real but so is Your grace. Bring such grace that mother and daughter both find healing; bring such grace that the next days fill with possibilities; bring such grace that we find our worth in having been created in Your image, Father, Son, Holy Spirit, so that in all things we give You the praise. Amen.

Elderly

Giving Up Housekeeping

Whether it is a decision to leave "the old home place" or a decision to enter an assisted living facility, the pain looms large when such choices have to be made.

Example

Rachel Redmond lived in the same house for thirty-two years. She and her husband had moved there together (our first real house), and she had stayed there for the thirty years after their divorce. It was "Granny's Place" for three grandchildren. It was surrounded by a community of long-time neighbors. It was, in brief, home. The house itself was large and maintaining it was difficult. "Maybe I need a smaller place, an apartment. But I just hate to leave here."

> Even the sparrow finds a home,
> and the swallow a nest for herself,
> where she may lay her young,
> at your altars, O LORD of hosts,
> my King and my God. (Psalm 84:3)

Prayer

O God, Whose love is really our dwelling place, these are times of decision about a house made with hands that has become a home filled with remembrance. Move among us that Your wisdom and Your will may prevail. Protect us from the shallow places of our reasoning and give us daring to dig deeply within ourselves.

In our hearts now, O God, good competes with good. There is value in this good place; there is also value in a different kind of tomorrow. Help us sort through the "what has been's" with celebration and sadness; help us sort through the "what can be's" with hope and dream.

Guide Your child Rachel. Give her the assurance that You dwell in houses, in apartments, in condos, in care facilities; You dwell even on the streets. Guard her best thinking so that distractions may lose their hold on her. Govern her emotions so that with balance she moves with clarity toward next day, next month, next year.

Holy Comforter, You have not brought us this far just to leave us behind, so we make petition upon Your presence so that in this and in all things, there may be strength for Your people and glory for Your name; through the saving grace of the triune God. Amen.

E L D E R L Y

VOLUNTEERING

As persons move beyond responsibilities of job and family duties, new opportunities for volunteer service open up.

Example

A.S.K. (Active Seniors Karing) was an organization of retired persons at St. Timothy Church. To date, they had completed two Habitat for Humanity projects and had made a mission trip to Costa Rica. Their fifteen members reported more than forty-two volunteer connections: Red Cross, day care center, ushering at cultural events, activity in community theater, tutoring, hospital receptionist, surrogate grandparents—the list went on. To celebrate these outreach and witness ministries, St. Timothy Church held a church-wide dinner in honor of A.S.K. (Four members of A.S.K. could not attend because they were out of town helping a flood recovery program.)

> *"When locks are long in Israel,*
> *when the people offer themselves willingly—*
> *bless the LORD!" (Judges 5:2)*

Prayer

(After each petition, you are invited to respond, "Lord, we give You thanks.")

For the bounty of lives lived fully: "Lord, we give You thanks."

For those who care and love and share: "Lord, we give You thanks."

For places where we are needed: "Lord, we give You thanks."

For times when energy and hope meet: "Lord, we give You thanks."

For these and all signs of Your mercy: "Lord, we give You thanks."

Eternal God, the same from everlasting to everlasting, You have blessed this congregation with examples of well-lived lives. You have given us mothers and fathers in the faith who continue to nurture their children by word and by deed. Already You have touched this group with power and have provided us with human echoes of One Who said, "Ask and it shall be given."

For gifts yet ungiven: "Lord, we give You thanks."

For mission still to come: "Lord, we give You thanks."

For the living power of Christ Jesus: "Lord, we give You thanks." Amen.

PATRIOTIC OCCASIONS
DEPLOYMENT OF MILITARY

A lthough military personnel understand that deployment into settings of war is part of job and duty, such separation from family and security is difficult. Both the deployed armed forces and those kin and friends who are left behind have major adjustments to make.

Example

Knowing that at some unknown time in the near future, the very near future, Captain Baskin would be sent to the active war zone, family members tried to live normal lives. It was not easy. Although some of them wondered if the cause justified this investment of men and women, most acknowledged and appreciated the sense of patriotic commitment, which had first led Harry Baskin to enlist and which now gave him a sense of purpose.

> All these were the sons of Jediael according to the heads of their ancestral houses, mighty warriors, seventeen thousand two hundred, ready for service in war. (1 Chronicles 7:11)

Prayer

God of peace, how we Your children work in stumbles and starts to find the way to peace! God of justice, how we Your children mix blind eyes and clear vision as we seek to name justice! God of possibilities, how we Your children close and open doors in order to find the possibilities You have for us!

Your child Harry now offers himself as an instrument of peace, justice, and possibility. We are grateful that he has such love for home, for country. We are grateful that he has such commitment to duty, to responsibility. Even so, we dare not send him on his own, but always in Your attentive care.

Be with us all as we are apart from one another. Send forth the same sunshine to reach us here and to reach Harry there. Receive our anxieties, our fears, our doubts, our pride, our hope, our courage, and always our readiness to serve You. Hear us pray for our enemies. Reshape the broken places in Your creation until we can study war no more. No more. And until then, fill us all with peace within; through Jesus Christ our Lord. Amen.

CONSCIENTIOUS OBJECTOR

One of the remarkable freedoms offered in the United States is one's right to declare oneself a conscientious objector to military service. When one understands such a declaration to be God's will, the decision becomes one of priorities and of patriotism: how my country is best in God's intent.

Example

Spence King's neighbors often wondered why the teen would go into his front yard each morning and raise the family's American flag. "I guess he is just patriotic," they said. Indeed, he was. Spence was grateful to live in a country that gave him freedom of conscience. Conscience was what his Uncle Clint called "listening to the most important voice." When Spence listened to that voice, he found it clearest in the words and life of Jesus. So when it came time to register with the Selective Service System, Spence recalled Jesus' plea that people know the things that make for peace and Jesus' assertion that peacemakers are blessed. "Others see it differently," he said, "but for me that means that I must say no to war."

As he came near and saw the city, he wept over it, saying, "If you, even you, had only recognized on this day the things that make for peace! But now they are hidden from your eyes." (Luke 19:41-42)

Prayer

O God, Who finds pleasure in the obedience of Your people, we praise You that You have planted in the heart of Spence King the desire to obey Your holy will. He sees and hears Your purposes in a way that seems strange to some, but we praise You for a nation that gives him a place to stand and the liberty of voice to say yes to Your intention for peace.

Give Spence the courage to hold fast to his convictions, but bless him also with a kind awareness of those who disagree with him and who even protect his right to conscience. In the community of this nation, Spence protects us from unalloyed commitment to war, even as others, in their way, guard and serve us with weapons.

Teach us who in all these ways yearn for peace; teach us to live together in peace and respect and trust. In the name of the One Whose birth was announced as "peace on earth," even our Lord Jesus Christ. Amen.

PATRIOTIC OCCASIONS

VETERANS' DAY

Over the years, millions have answered a call to serve country. For some, it was a call to death. For some, it was a call to broken body or spirit. For some, it was a call to wait. For some, it was a call to purpose. Veterans Day honors those men and women.

Example

Josephine Walking Horse wanted to be in the Marines ever since she learned that her father died (when she was two) in a military plane crash. "I'll take his place," she said. The experiences of war soon lost all glamour for her as she lived in the hard places of innocent victims, enemy fire lines, mortal decisions, and children—all the hurting children. When she returned home, she wanted to close off that part of her life. But once a year, Josephine emerged from her protective cocoon to remember those who had fought because they thought a fight was necessary. "On Veterans Day," she said to no one in particular, "I always wonder where God was in all that."

> Proclaim this among the nations:
> Prepare war,
>   stir up the warriors.
> Let all the soldiers draw near,
>   let them come up. (Joel 3:9)

Prayer

O God, Who suffers when any of Your children suffer, we thank You for walking with us in the complex places of life. We are refreshed by the bravery and sacrifice You have planted in our hearts and are moved by those whose love of home, neighbor, and country has so fully expended that sacrifice and bravery. Such is a gift from You.

Forgive us when we confuse Your love for us with a pride of thinking You love only us. Forgive us when we take satisfaction in the destruction that war accumulates. But give us joy when evil is overcome and freedom is protected.

In this land and in other lands, women and men have taken up the banner of battle, suffering in victory and in defeat over the causes that divide us. Thank You for those remembered on this day as persons of justice, freedom, and service—the boundaries that honor You.

For veterans who served in action, for veterans who served in support, for veterans who served in preparing, for veterans who served with life and limb, for veterans who served in objection, we give You thanks. Keep the canopy of care over us and over all Your children. Amen.

HOSPITAL

FACING A TEST

Even routine tests can cause anxiety: "What if there is something there no one knows about!" Medical lab work can be frightening if there has been even a hint of a severe problem.

Example

Francis Felton did not usually make pastoral visits to Mercy Hospital at 5:00 in the morning, but last night Ron Rappaport called: "Reverend, pray for Nora; she is very worried about that test they are going to run at Mercy first thing tomorrow morning. We don't think it is anything, but then you never know."

> *As a mother comforts her child,*
> *so I will comfort you;*
> *you shall be comforted in Jerusalem. (Isaiah 66:13)*

Prayer

Eternal God, through all the ages You have shown us that You want what is best for Your children. Thank You for keeping us within the shadow of Your wings. And thank You for those whose place of study and ministry is such that they can test and probe and think in ways that lead to the best decisions for us. Use these doctors and nurses and technicians as instruments of Your work of health.

Be with Nora as she moves toward these hours of uncertainty. Set her free from distracting distress. Claim her fully as Your child and, with the embracing warmth of a mother, comfort her.

We thank You for all the ways You have brought Nora to this moment and to this good place of care and health. And we dare to assert even now the confidence that tomorrow will be no stranger for You, but will be a time when Your yes will still be yes and Your grace will still be sufficient.

For the mark of baptism, which is not erased by our circumstance, we praise Your generous Name. For the table where we have been fed for such a time as this, we praise Your renewing power. In the name of the One who gave us a glimpse of Your kingdom where all are healed, even Jesus Christ our Lord. Amen.

H O S P I T A L

FACING SURGERY

There is a saying that few surgeries are significant unless they happen to be on you! "Being put to sleep," "getting cut on," "painful, uncertain recovery" each brings its own intrusion of dread.

Example

"Elaine," began Jerri English, speaking to her new pastor, "you don't know me very well. I am not someone who usually gets worried, but I've got to tell you that I am scared, scared, scared about this surgery. I know I am right with God, at least I think I am, but I know I am not ready to leave my family." Elaine West noticed the tears that began to slip down the face of her parishioner. "It's the not knowing that is driving me up the wall!"

And the peace of God, which surpasses all understanding, will guard your hearts and your minds in Christ Jesus. (Philippians 4:7)

Prayer

God of all times, this too is a day You have made and we shall rejoice and be glad in it. We lift up and magnify Your name for the goodness that has led us to places of care, that has brought us to physicians of Your healing mercy, that has surrounded us with family and faith friends.

You have taught us to bear one another's burdens, so now we take on the concern and insecurity felt by Your child Jerri. We take it on so we can offer it to You that You might touch our weakness with Your power, our brokenness with Your healing, and our faith with Your saving.

Watch over those who become Your hands during this surgery. Bless them with clarity and calmness. Unite this team of doctors, nurses, orderlies, and staff so they can undertake this ministry with oneness.

And peace—we ask for peace for Jerri. Pour upon her that peace that the world cannot give, that the world cannot understand, and, praise Your name, that the world cannot take away. All of this is in the name of the healing, holy One, Jesus Christ. Amen.

H O S P I T A L

LOSS OF A LIMB

Life changes after an amputation. Often, one can slowly return to life's regular flow, but the operative word is *slowly*. The physical shock to one's system might well be matched by the spiritual shock to one's assurance.

Example

The irony is that Caswell Smith returned from a war zone without so much as a bruise. Now, he twisted in his hospital bed at Northern Medical Center, knowing that when next he woke up, he would not have a right leg. The motorcycle accident had destroyed any possibility of saving the limb. He called upon all of his bravery and stretched his imagination to its fullest, but it was still hard to see how "I'm going to be worth much tomorrow."

> The LORD is near to the brokenhearted,
> and saves the crushed in spirit. (Psalm 34:18)

Prayer

Why, O God, why has this bitter brokenness visited Your child Caswell?

How, O God, how are the days ahead to include fullness of life?

When, O God, when will this ache, both within and without, go away?

Where, O God, where can we turn for direction, for help?

Who, O God, who can be trusted in a world like this?

Thank You, Word that became flesh, that You hear our questions! Thank You, Word that spoke and created, that You promise new creation. Thank You, Word that breathes to make us human, that You give us wholeness.

There is grief, O Master, in this loss of limb. And we know that You grieved when Your friends grieved. In Your resurrection power, You have moved us from despair to hope, from defeat to victory, from death to life.

We don't pretend to set aside the mystery painted by life's strange brush, but we claim a good tomorrow for Caswell because we claim Your presence in it. Because we see Jesus Christ, we see life made whole. Move us from this hard now as the very beginning point of Your comforting, healing time to come. In Christ's name, we pray. Amen.

H O S P I T A L

FAMILY WAITING

The patient is asleep in surgery, and now it is the family's turn to wait. "When will they tell us something?" "How long is this supposed to take?" "How soon will we be able to see him?" "Why is this taking so long?" "Do you think he will recognize us?"

Example

Sam Daughtry and Neal Isley had lived together for eleven years, so when Neal went into University Hospital for major surgery, both the Daughtry family and the Isley family gathered in the ICU waiting room. The clock's slow tick almost seemed to mock their impatience for some word from the doctors. Two hours. Three hours. Four hours. The idle, time-filling chitchat had long since run out. Sam tried to read the eyes of his pastor for some clue: is this kind of wait normal?

Let us therefore approach the throne of grace with boldness, so that we may receive mercy and find grace to help in time of need. (Hebrews 4:16)

Prayer

It is hard to wait. Even in Your presence, dear Lord, it is hard to wait. Help us let go of our need to control. In our love and care for Neal, we find it difficult to turn him over to You and to those women and men who even now live out the expectation we have placed upon them.

We praise You for the blessings we already see: families joined in common interest, life lived well together, Your love of Neal in baptismal covenant, the healing ministries of this place, and the hope-filled, caring spirits that enter now into these moments, these long, long moments of waiting.

Hear now the silent prayer of each heart. (*Pause for silent prayer.*)

Take care of Neal, gracious God; take care of Neal. In Christ's holy name, Amen.

H O S P I T A L

EMERGENCY ROOM

Hospital stays have a unique stress, but there is an accelerated strain about trips to the emergency room. Here the anxiety of waiting, the uncertainty of diagnosis, the suddenness of circumstances, and the unfamiliarity of procedure and people blur into the surreal.

Example

"Bob, forget the ball game," Pastor Hilbert heard on his cell phone. His wife continued, "The Soto family just called; Raoul has been taken to the emergency room at St. Catherine's Hospital. They don't know what is wrong. They said they just wanted you to know so you could pray for him, but I think they really want you to come to the hospital." Bob Hilbert took one last look at the scoreboard (Home 32, Visitors 29) and moved toward the exit.

God is faithful; by him you were called into the fellowship of his Son, Jesus Christ our Lord. (1 Corinthians 1:9)

Prayer

None of us expected to be here tonight, O Holy God, but none of us is surprised to find that You are already here. You go where Your people hurt. You go where Your people wonder. You go where Your people wait. Thank you for that grace, which precedes us to all of life's surprises.

Around us, Lord, are many people suddenly caught up in illness, accident, even the unknown. Here is loneliness; here is anger; here is guilt; here is doubt; here is hope against hope; here is waiting; there is waiting. Even if others cannot name Your presence, comfort their hearts and calm their thoughts.

Raoul is Yours. We are glad that You have made him part of our lives, but first he was Yours; still he is Yours. Walk with him on this unclear path, so with Your hand on his, he might step with confidence into new places. Restore him to the fullness that You can give; through Jesus Christ, the Healer. Amen.

H O S P I T A L

ORGAN DONATION

Families, still in the midst of the first wave of grief, often face decisions about whether or not to donate the organs of a deceased loved one.

Example

The loss came suddenly, Xavier Morton's body broken beyond recovery in the fall from the treacherous mountain trail. "He was young and in good shape," said the doctor, "but the damage was too much, even for him." Now, Xavier's parents looked at the words on their son's driver's license, "organ donor," and realized that they would have to decide. There was little time for reflection. Carmen Morton asked the doctor, "Do I have time to call my pastor and ask him to pray with me over the phone?"

> But Peter said, "I have no silver or gold, but what I have I give you; in the name of Jesus Christ of Nazareth, stand up and walk." (Acts 3:6)

Prayer

Come, Lord Jesus, into this hurting place. Into these moments of shock, even disbelief, come with healing grace. Come, Lord Jesus, and cry with us. Come with Your resurrection power for this young disciple of Yours, Xavier.

We thank You for his life, his ready engagement with the green of Your creation, his love of the out-of-doors. We thank You for his energy, which gave us the fullness of his affection and his total commitment to whatever task was at hand. We thank You that we loved him enough to miss him already.

Now, stay with the Mortons as they spend time in the hard place of decision. Help them write with clear strokes that which can be Xavier's continuing gift. Grant them the peace to search their deepest reservoirs of tenderness. Open their eyes to the fullest memory of their son.

We pray for wisdom while under pressure. We pray for judgment while enveloped by grief. We pray for discernment while pulled in many ways. Grant us an assurance, by the fullness of Your goodness, that whatever choice is made may become the beginning mark of Your abiding comfort; through Jesus Christ our Lord. Amen.

H O S P I T A L

RECEIVING ORGAN DONATION

A lthough the wait may have been long, the time to act is usually brief. Those who are to receive a potential new lease on life because of an organ donation feel anxiety, gratitude, and wonder.

Example

The Reverend Judy Wise drove quickly through the night streets to get to Memorial Medical Center. The massive brick building and its seemingly endless hallways appeared to swallow her up as she rushed to room 4233. Donning protective gown and mask, she went in to see Burt Creighton. Already, the tubes and wires running to Burt's frail body signaled that it would not be long until he would be wheeled down to Operating Suite Three, the site of heart transplant surgery. Ms. Wise was not even sure that Burt could hear her, but she began to pray.

> *Jesus said to him, "Stand up, take your mat and walk." At once the man was made well, and he took up his mat and began to walk. (John 5:8-9)*

Prayer

Our heavenly Father, the slow pages of our calendar have turned to this day, to this moment. We release Burt Creighton into Your care. You have moved a kind spirit in some family we do not know to make available a heart that could bring quality back into Burt's days among us. We praise Your name for such a gift. We are awed by the creative power You work through physicians and other agents of healing. Put Your maternal touch upon them that the birth of this generous giving may be the birth of new possibilities for Burt.

Take the force of our fears and turn it into the power of hope. Take the weakness we bring to this time and meet it with Your strength. Take the numbness of our waiting and turn it into the liveliness of possibility. All of this we ask as we give You the praise; through the Master, Jesus Christ. Amen.

H O S P I T A L

ENDING LIFE SUPPORT

When patients move beyond the possibility of recovery and have no life quality beyond machine, family members and doctors together worry about decisions to remove the systems of life support. A pastor who has been visiting regularly will probably be aware when such a choice has to be made.

Example

Charity Kim's brother and sister did not agree. One argued, "She would never want to be kept alive this way, if you call this alive!" The other retorted, "It still seems like we are just giving up and not giving her every chance!" The doctors at Wilkinson Center Hospital had given careful medical opinions: no brain wave activity, no independent body functions. "If we take away the support systems, nature will run its course in a few days, maybe a few hours." Three days later, Charity's brother and sister, with medical power of attorney, gave permission to withhold the machines.

If we live, we live to the Lord, and if we die, we die to the Lord; so then, whether we live or whether we die, we are the Lord's. (Romans 14:8)

Prayer

Eternal God, the Parent of all our love, we simply shrink before the mystery of life and death. For a season, You have given us Charity, and we are thankful for her good place in our lives. We are also thankful that we can let go of our hold on her and release her into Your fuller care. You have created us to be stewards of one another, and we pray that You will brush with grace the decision here made.

In Your hands are our beginning and our end. Living, we are Yours. Dying, we are Yours. In baptismal waters, You made covenant promise that Charity would always be Your child. You are a God Who keeps promises, so we praise You from whom all blessings flow.

For this brother and sister who have anguished to make holy choices, we thank You. For the sturdiness of family bonds, we thank You. For the places You prepare at Your banquet table, we thank You.

We can love because You first loved us and in that awareness, we pray, as we have been taught: "Our Father . . . "

M I S C E L L A N E O U S

CONVERSION

The Christian journey is about transformation. For some persons, the change is remarkably sudden—such as Paul on the road to Damascus. For others, the renovation has come more gently—such as Timothy's nurturing by his mother and grandmother. However God works this miracle, life is different with the recognition of the claim of Jesus Christ upon it!

Example

Pastor Dell wondered why Creech Whitaker lingered after the service. Mr. Whitaker had attended every night of the series of Lenten services, but never seemed to have anything more to say than "Well, Preacher, I'll see you tomorrow night." After everyone else had gone, the two stood in the only hallway of the small church. "Good to see you, Creech," Dr. Dell began, but the middle-aged merchant interrupted. "I'm a direct, plain-speaking man," he said, "so let me just say it: I want to give my life to Jesus."

> Now as he was going along and approaching Damascus, suddenly a light from heaven flashed around him. (Acts 9:3)

> I am reminded of your sincere faith, a faith that lived first in your grandmother Lois and your mother Eunice and now, I am sure, lives in you. (2 Timothy 1:5)

Prayer

Lord and Savior, how remarkable are Your gifts of repentance and salvation and holy living! Your servant Creech comes now because You have worked a gift into his life, a gift of faith, a gift of change, a gift of new beginning. Thank You for not letting go until Creech said "Yes!" Hear this prayer, O God of new creation.

(Creech, if these words reflect your own heart, repeat these prayers after me.)

Lord God, for years I have hidden from the fullness of what You would give me. (*Pause*) I have tried life on my own without much more than a nod of appreciation to You. (*Pause*) And You have kept on loving me. (*Pause*) I declare my sin. (*Pause*) I accept You as my Savior from that sin. (*Pause*) I declare my life of fragments. (*Pause*) I accept You as the Lord of my life. (*Pause*) Thank You, Lord Jesus. Thank You, Lord Jesus. (*Pause*) Amen.

GIVING UP SMOKING

Turning from bad habits and imprisoning addictions is not easy. When some persons decide to give up smoking, they quit "cold turkey." Others find assistance in over-the-counter or prescription aids. In almost all cases, cessation of smoking is more likely if there are relationships of accountability.

Example

Marshall Young and his wife, Monique Bass, wanted to stop smoking. "We want to have children, and we do not want them to grow up in a house that reeks of smoke," Monique said rather straightforwardly. The young couple sat in the pastor's study at Bridgeton Church. "And we know that we are not giving God a very good chance of giving us health!" Marshall added. Pastor Washington said, "Let's name five other people you are going to tell about this, and then let's all get together for a prayer of commitment."

> The LORD is my light and my salvation;
> whom shall I fear?
> The LORD is the stronghold of my life;
> of whom shall I be afraid? (Psalm 27:1)

Prayer

You have created us for well-being, compassionate God, but we have sometimes wasted Your creation. You have made us for others, loving God, but we have sometimes been willing to settle for self. You have created us for freedom, holy God, but we have sometimes chosen harm instead of health. Hear the confession we make this day.

(*Invite Marshall and Monique to confess their tobacco addiction*) Forgiving God, we are ready for a new beginning. These Your servants Marshall and Monique seek Your strength for turning around. Help them break the bars of tobacco's prison. Cleanse their bodies and minds of the residue of smoke. Take away the desires that hurt them and, as those desires leave, grant them courage and patience.

We praise You for these who have entered into a covenant with Marshall and Monique, sharing this journey of newness. We have seen in Jesus Christ that You make all things new, so even now we mark this as a time of fresh start.

(*Invite all to join hands in a circle.*) Now, as we go forth from this time of commitment, send us out with the assurance that we do not go alone. These friends are a sign of Your love, which will not let us go. For this and for the victory, we give You praise. Amen.

Miscellaneous

Controversial Issues

Name the subject: abortion, homosexuality, capital punishment, war, economic policy, genetic technology, or divorce. Christians have heard God speak differently on these matters. Sometimes there is space for these variations; sometimes little, if any, room is allowed for difference.

Example

A small group gathered in the basement of Westside Church. The Reverend Lamont Clarkson had asked them to meet with him: "Is there any way we can stay in dialogue even as we disagree?" Betty Kent said, "I hate to say it, but my Bible is too clear on the subject for me to have much to talk about." Arch Garber spoke up: "I think we read the same Bible, Betty. I just think you might have missed a few verses . . . you know, the ones about love!" They did agree to pray together before they left.

> For I fear that when I come, I may find you not as I wish, and that you may find me not as you wish; I fear that there may perhaps be quarreling, jealousy, anger, selfishness, slander, gossip, conceit, and disorder. (2 Corinthians 12:20)

Prayer

God of the prophets, You have called Your people to be Your messengers. We seek the truth of Your Word so we can proclaim with clarity, but we confess that we have not always sought the love in Your Word so we can proclaim with charity.

God of the saints, You have called Your people to live holy lives. We look to tradition to see the path of those who came before us, but we confess that we have not always seen the trails that ran side by side.

God of the mind, You have called Your people to transparency of thought. We look to reason to put life together in some coherent, meaningful way; but we confess that we have sometimes turned our backs on mystery and revelation.

God of the now, You have called Your people to personal relationships with You. We look to experience with gratitude, but we confess that we have sometimes blinded ourselves to the life You intended for us to have together.

O Spirit, Who inspired the Holy Word, You live among us now. Inspire that Word again within our hearts, within our minds, within our lives; through the one Savior of us all, even Jesus Christ our Lord. Amen.

PRISONER BEING EXECUTED

Persons who are to suffer the death penalty have the option of some final moments with a clergyperson of their choice. It is hard to imagine a setting in which every word carries such weight and every prayer carries such hope.

Example

Some editorials referred to Johnson Berry's recent death row claim of faith as a calculated effort to argue for leniency from the courts. Others sneered that it was probably just "a little insurance." Chaplain Metcalf was not so cynical. Over a period of years, he had seen the working of the Holy Spirit in the damaged life of the convicted murderer. When the final legal recourse ended any prospect of life, Mr. Berry said, "I've never denied I killed that man. And I knew better. God, forgive me. God gives new beginnings, and I guess mine will be in heaven."

I have come to call not the righteous but sinners to repentance. (Luke 5:32)

Prayer

You must not be through with miracles, O God, because You have gotten through hardness of heart to find Your child Johnson. Thank You for the saving power of Jesus Christ. In His death, our sin has already died. In His resurrection, our new life has already begun.

We come to a time now, loving God, when all we can carry with us is Your promise. We can cling to nothing of our doing, but we cling to Your promise. We can face only the powers of execution, but we can face it with Your promise. We can see only an eternity, but we can see it with Your promise.

Nothing done here this day will erase Your love of Johnson. Nothing done here this day will lessen his acceptance of Your love. So now grant Johnson a peace that this world has not given, but, praise be Your name, that this world cannot take away.

And in a final unity with Your Son and in a final oneness with all Your saints, we pray as Jesus taught His friends to pray: "Our Father . . . "

PERSON LIVING WITH AIDS

Stigma and fear still surround those who are living with AIDS. The weakening from illness is underlined by harsh judgments by many in society.

Example

"What bothers me as much as this illness is the assumptions that everyone makes about me." Reggie Berini was talking passionately with his pastor. Reggie paused for a moment and then lifted his head from the pillow. "Reverend, they say that God is punishing me. Those folks don't know a thing about me and what I have done or not done or what I have prayed or not prayed. The way they talk is almost enough to make me dislike God!" The Reverend Ms. Maxton waited for a moment, not wanting to speak too hastily. She reached out and took Reggie's hand.

Cast all your anxiety on him, because he cares for you. (1 Peter 5:7)

Prayer

Our best view of You, Holy God, is through the lens of Christ Jesus. And through His life, death, resurrection, ascension, and promised return, we see a grace that lets nothing separate us from Your love. Our own self-doubts may shatter our peace, but You still love us. The distaste that others have for us may hurt our core, but You still love us. The ravages of illness may weaken our resolve, but You still love us.

Out of that love, You call us to times of confession, to times of forgiveness, to times of silence, to times of witness, to times of hope. Clear our lives of bitterness that there might be more room for joy. Clear our lives of despair that there might be more room for expectation. Clear our lives of sin that there might be more room for victory.

Keep Reggie supported with Your presence, even when he does not feel it. Keep Reggie sustained by Your peace, even when he does not taste it. Keep Reggie as Your child, even when he does not know it. This is what we see in Jesus Christ, so we pray in His name. Amen.

MISCELLANEOUS

50TH WEDDING ANNIVERSARY

More than family can celebrate when a couple remains married for half a century! It is a community delight for something special.

Example

When Fred Voight and Para Makula got married, no one expected that the couple would have to go through three job losses, two times of international war, the death of a child, the divorce of a grandchild, near bankruptcy, and a house burning to the ground! Fred and Para did not expect it either, but they did expect to face it all together. Fifty years. "We made it by being two different people facing in the same direction," Fred said. "That's true," Para teased, "but a few times I had to turn Fred so he would be facing in the right direction!" The crowd in the packed church fellowship hall laughed and applauded. Fifty years.

So they are no longer two, but one flesh. Therefore what God has joined together, let no one separate. (Matthew 19:6)

Prayer

With thanksgiving, we come before You today grateful for Fred and Para. Day upon day, year upon year, decade upon decade, they have walked the hills and the valleys of marriage. They have worked to be two candles giving one light. And in all things, they have lifted up Your name!

The sunshine of Your presence has given light when daily tasks and world agenda gave darkness. And, in all times, they have been open to new leadings of Your Spirit.

We are not so foolish, O God, as to think that these have been perfect years. Some memories of death, loss, and pain challenge us. Some signs of mistakes and even selfishness have clouded the day. But, in all turns, they have seen Your love as sufficient.

Already, we reach for more years, O God, more than a mere fifty! We praise You for a couple who has worn both victory and loss with dignity and with an eye on the One who would bring light, Jesus our Lord. Move us toward an eternity that You have begun here, now. And in even this, Fred and Para move on in gladness.

For children (*have each child call out his or her name*), for grandchildren (*have each grandchild call out his or her name*), for us all, we say, "Joyful, joyful, we adore You, God of glory, Lord of Love." Amen.

SCENE OF AN ACCIDENT

A pastor may just "happen" to be near the scene of a wreck or an industrial accident; a pastor may be called to come to the place of such a mishap. In either case, either privately or publicly, the pastor can express a prayer.

Example

The parsonage household piled into the car and headed for the beach. School's out! Vacation! Before long, they were zipping with the traffic on the interstate highway. Only ten miles from the coast, Pastor Chadwick saw the telltale signal of taillights, one after another blipping red, and soon he too stopped. People seemed to be getting out of their cars to see what the problem might be. Mr. Chadwick walked a few steps toward the scene, turned, and told his children to wait in the car. He got close enough to see that the crash had destroyed two cars and gravely injured at least three or four people. "Good Samaritans" were offering assistance to the victims of the accident. In the distance was the sound of an approaching emergency vehicle. The pastor knelt by the side of the road. He prayed aloud. When he looked up, he was surprised to see five strangers kneeling beside him.

> Hear my prayer, O LORD;
> let my cry come to you.
> Do not hide your face from me
> in the day of my distress.
> Incline your ear to me;
> answer me speedily in the day when I call. (Psalm 102:1-2)

Prayer

God of all peoples, some of Your children are hurting. I cannot put them before You by name; but in the wealth of Your love, You know them. I cannot even know what has happened to them; but to the fullness of Your care, I commit them. Some lives have been changed, O God, and Your steady hand is needed.

Give them peace, even if they do not know Who gave it. Grant tenderness to those who now minister to them. And bring with haste and safety those who come to help.

I cannot say how these people call You by name nor do I know if they pray at all; but I bring You this prayer in the name of One Who heals, my Lord, my Savior, Jesus Christ. Amen.

BLESSING OF A HOME

B e it an apartment, a dormitory room, a suburban duplex, a newly con-
structed dream house, a restored family place, a three-story mansion,
or a bed in the community shelter, it can be home. For Christians, part of
what makes a place into a home is the blessing of God upon the people
there.

Example

For years, Janette O'Brian had dreamed of having her own house. This
goal, however, was beyond the range of her "teacher" pocketbook. As she
shared her vision with a colleague at the school, Korin Baker, the light
went on for both of them at the same time! Let's buy a house together!
"We'll get one with some common spaces and some separate spaces and a
two-car garage!" For several months, the two friends spent weekends
checking out false leads on "just the right house." It was Korin who spotted
8724 Brewster Drive. Good separate space for each. Good common space
for both. And the two-car garage! No wonder that Korin invited her pastor and Janette invited her pastor to bless this new home.

> The LORD bless you and keep you;
> the LORD make his face to shine upon you, and be gracious to you;
> the LORD lift up his countenance upon you, and give you peace.
> (Numbers 6:24-26)

Prayer

All glory be to Your name, O God, that in Your triune presence You
have brought Korin and Janette to this day of happiness. You have been
with them as they came to this sheltering place and in thanksgiving they
offer You lives of service.

Bless the daily pace of this home. When there is joy, may it be mutual.
When there is sorrow, may it be shared. When there is disagreement, may
it be open. Bring holiness and righteousness and justice and mercy into the
witness of Korin and Janette.

Friendship can be sorely tested by closeness, O God, so guide these
friends into respect for distinct lives. In blessing these two, Creator God,
You bless the students they teach, the colleagues with whom they work,
and all who will be touched by their spirit of renewal, made possible by
this shared house. Make it a home with Your abiding Spirit; through Jesus
Christ, we pray. Amen.

MISCELLANEOUS

BALL GAME

In some areas of the country, prayers are offered before athletic events. (Keep in mind that in this writer's part of the United States, they would mean praying for Blue Devils and Demon Deacons!) Some teams have pastors who are part of the pre-game routine.

Example

The last time Eastway High School played North City High School, the football game exploded into a near riot. Each side blamed the others for the outburst. As players left the field after the game, some taunted others with threats "to even things up next year." Rather than cancel this week's game between EHS and NCHS, school officials developed several unusual measures, including asking pastors to include prayers for the game during their weekly worship services.

> And the streets of the city shall be full of boys and girls playing in its streets. Thus says the LORD of hosts: Even though it seems impossible to the remnant of this people in these days, should it also seem impossible to me, says the LORD of hosts? (Zechariah 8:5-6)

Prayer

O merciful God, part of Your vision of a city at peace is youth playing together. We celebrate Your gift of sports as a way of growth, a way of challenge, a way of excitement, and a way of new friendships. We thank You for creating us so that silly things we do with a pigskin can be fun!

We confess that sometimes we take ourselves too seriously. We acknowledge before Your throne of truth that sometimes we have let the pride we have in our school become a weapon of anger. Forgive us when we steal from Your pleasure in good things, when we make something hurtful out of Your gift of sport.

Protect us from us, when we are at our worst. Watch over the athletes as they seek to do their best. And keep us all in the joy of living as Christ would have us live, for we pray in His name. Amen.